Railways and Tra
in the City of Leeas

Above: The final development of steam locomotive for hauling the crack ex-LNER express trains were the Class 'A1' 4-6-2s, a number of which were based at Copley Hill for operating the London trains. Here No 60133 *Pommern* stops at Holbeck High Level with the up 'Yorkshire Pullman' in 1951. *E. R. Morten collection*

Below: After the end of steam diesels took over the principal trains from Leeds to London King's Cross. Class 40, 44 and 47 locomotives were used at first, while a batch of 'Deltic' locomotives were specially built for these trains, which they operated until 1979. No 55007 *Pinza* heads a train for London at Leeds station in 1975. *Author*

Railways and Tramways in the City of Leeds

Alan J. Haigh

Silver Link Publishing Ltd

© Alan J. Haigh 2010

ISBN 978 1 85794 333 7

Silver Link Publishing Ltd
The Trundle
Ringstead Road
Great Addington
Kettering
Northants NN14 4BW

Tel/Fax: 01536 330588
email: sales@nostalgiacollection.com
Website: www.nostalgiacollection.com

Printed and bound in the Czech Republic

First published in 2010

British Library Cataloguing in Publication Data

A catalogue record for this book is available from the British Library.

Acknowledgements

The author would like to thank all the many people, too numerous to mention, who helped with this work, which is based upon experiences and information noted and collected over the past 50 years. However, special thanks are due to the staff at Leeds Public Library for their patience in helping me research old maps, Acts of Parliament and local history, as well as to those who so willingly provided photographs.

Further reading

Joy, David *A Regional History of the Railways of Great Britain, Volume 8: South and West Yorkshire*
Soper, J. *Leeds Transport, Volumes 1, 2, 3 and 4* (Leeds Transport Historical Society)
Young, Andrew D. *Leeds Trams, 1932-1959* (Light Railway Transport League)
Acts of Parliament
Bradshaw and railway company timetables
Ordnance Survey maps, 1:2500
The Railway Magazine, 1897 to date

Contents

Preface

An up-to-date look at the railways and tramways of Leeds in one volume is long overdue. The city was a pioneer in engineering and railway development with a complicated and ever-changing network of lines.

In order to avoid unnecessary and repetitive accounts of these changes they have been recorded in mainly tabular and diagrammatic forms, together with the extensive use of photographs. Sketch maps of all the stations and major junctions have been included; as most have now disappeared, these show their extent and location. It has not been possible to draw these to scale because of the linear nature of railways, but these are represented as near as possible to show the general railway scene. The diagrams also show the track layouts in as much detail as possible, although for some of the most extensive railway centres some minor lines and sidings have been omitted. Where possible north is to the top of the page.

An attempt has been made to show the extent of goods depots and sidings, but not all were open at the same time; for example, collieries were continually closing as their coal seams became exhausted. Generally, however, most freight facilities were closed down in the period 1955 to 1975.

The present boundaries of the City of Leeds introduced in 1974 are used in this work. Prior to this Leeds grew from quite a small original settlement by progressively absorbing its smaller neighbours.

The Streamlined front end of a Eurostar high-speed train at Leeds station in 2002 as it forms a GNER service for London King's Cross. With talk in 2010 of plans to build new High Speed Line 2 from London to Leeds, this could be a regular sight in the future. *Author*

Introduction

In recent times no other similar-sized UK city has suffered from such poor public transport planning and development as the City of Leeds. Since the end of the Second World War a number of disastrous policies and decisions have deprived modern Leeds of adequate local railways and tramways to serve what is a major European city with a population of three-quarters of a million people, as well as being the regional centre of West and North Yorkshire.

Yet it was all so different in the early days of industrial Britain. Leeds was at the forefront of engineering, and the pioneering Middleton Railway was among the first to use rails for transporting coal. The arrival of main-line railways put Leeds at the centre of the railway network with lines to all parts of the country for transporting both freight and passengers. This was followed by the arrival of the city's tramways, initially horse-drawn then steam-powered, after which Leeds became a pioneer in developing electric tramways and trolleybuses.

These railways and tramways emerged to serve a city that was very densely populated around its centre, but with sparsely populated and mainly freestanding surrounding townships. As most people walked to work and were not affluent, the demand for travel was quite low and this was reflected in quite infrequent rail services with high fares, but within the city area there were more regular services on the tramway routes, which had very low fares.

Despite this, at the start of the 20th century Leeds had a comprehensive network of tramways and suburban railways. Additionally the vast majority of freight traffic was carried by the railways, with all engineering works and collieries connected to the network. In the centre of Leeds a large number of goods depots and warehouses sprang up to serve the movement of freight, and most suburban stations had goods traffic facilities.

The two World Wars and the inter-war years had little effect on the size of both the tramways and railways of Leeds. During the First World War the Government took control of the railways from 4 August 1914 until 22 September 1919. This control was exercised through a Railway Executive, the Chairman of which was the President of the Board of Trade, and which consisted of a committee composed of the General Managers of the individual railway companies.

The war had a profound effect on social life and the railway operations that had to cope with wartime regulations. There were reductions and decelerations of normal services, with some stations closed for the duration of the war. For, example, the London & North Western Railway (LNWR) station at Gildersome was closed from 1917 to 1919 and Churwell from 1917 to 1920. The railways had to carry much special traffic, including troops, ammunition and war material. They also had to cope with reductions in manpower as railwaymen enlisted; the North Eastern Railway (NER) lost 16% of its staff for this reason. More women were employed. Parliament passed the Summertime Act in 1916 to save fuel on lighting, with clocks put forward 1 hour between 20 May and 1 October. The war ended in 1918, but left the railways in a very run-down condition.

The tramways had similar problems with a shortage of staff and materials for maintaining the tramcars and tracks. Tramcar lighting was reduced to minimise the possibility of Zeppelin raids, although Leeds, unlike some other places, was not effected.

During the Second World War the railways again came under Government control, although this time the Railway Executive was a department of the Ministry of Transport.

The Executive was formed in 1938 and acquired full powers when war was declared. Operation of the railways was similar to the First World War, with reductions in passenger services, extended journey times and more freight carried. Unnecessary travel was discouraged, but despite this passenger journeys nationally increased from 1,225 million in 1939 to 1,371 million in 1943. A number of stations were closed permanently during the war, including Woodkirk, Churwell and Methley (LYR).

Leeds was fortunate in not being bombed as many times as other cities, with nine air raids in total, although the threat of bombing was always there. The worst attack was on the night of 9 March 1941 when up to 50 German aircraft attacked the city, many lives being lost and buildings damaged or destroyed.

The tramways were affected by blackout regulations and air raid precautions requiring modifications to lighting and provision of netting on tramcar windows. Swinegate Depot was hit in an air raid, but only five trams were damaged. To minimise the threat from bombing, at night trams were dispersed to suburban locations such as at Temple Newsam.

Two wars in just over 20 years had a drastic effect on both the tramways and railways, from which they never fully recovered. Modernisation and replacement of worn-out assets was delayed and when it finally came was too late to maintain previous services. Although at the end of the Second World War the city still had a comprehensive network of both, this was shortly about to change for the worse. The tramways were very run-down after serving the city well during the war years and the choice was between modernisation and abandonment; unfortunately the latter won the day. Local railways were in a similar position, but soldiered on with antiquated steam traction and rolling stock for a number of years until diesel units were introduced in the mid-1950s.

Social conditions began to change at this time, with slum clearances in the inner-city areas and massive building of new housing in east and south Leeds, as well as all the surrounding towns Collieries and factories were now starting to close, which, together with a rising population with more disposal income, resulted in a surge in demand for transport. All this should have been to the advantage of local train services, as commuting into Leeds was forecast to increase drastically. Despite this, national Government policy implemented the 'Beeching Report' of 1963, which closed most Leeds suburban railway stations.

Subsequently Leeds adopted a transport policy based almost exclusively on roads and began a programme of major new road building. At the time mail from Leeds was franked 'Leeds – Motorway City of the 1970s'.

As road traffic congestion increased it became clear that there needed to be a change in policy, and a number of efforts were made to reintroduce a modern tramway scheme and reopen suburban railway stations. To date little progress has been made in the provision of this much-needed 'light rail' system for Leeds, but a start has been made on reopening suburban stations, while long-distance and regional trains from Leeds have been greatly improved.

During the Second World War carriage and station posters were used to convey to the public wartime dangers and problems. The main message was the need to reduce unnecessary travelling. Another important subject was the dangers from the blackout. Carriages had passenger-operated slam doors, which remained on the railways until new rolling stock with guard-operated doors began to be introduced from 1984.

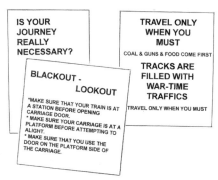

IS YOUR
JOURNEY
REALLY
NECESSARY?

TRAVEL ONLY
WHEN YOU
MUST

COAL & GUNS & FOOD COME FIRST

BLACKOUT -
LOOKOUT

*MAKE SURE THAT YOUR TRAIN IS AT
A STATION BEFORE OPENING
CARRIAGE DOOR.
* MAKE SURE YOUR CARRIAGE IS AT A
PLATFORM BEFORE ATTEMPTING TO
ALIGHT.
* MAKE SURE THAT YOU USE THE
DOOR ON THE PLATFORM SIDE OF
THE CARRIAGE.

TRACKS ARE
FILLED WITH
WAR-TIME
TRAFFICS

TRAVEL ONLY WHEN YOU MUST

1
The first railways

If we go back 250 years, water was the main means of transport and settlements were usually located on rivers. As the country became industrialised the demand for coal increased and some collieries were located away from this means of transport. Railways therefore emerged as wagonways to transport coal, and the Middleton Railway was the first to obtain an Act of Parliament for this purpose, in 1758. At first horse haulage was used, but the railway later joined with engineer Matthew Murray to pioneer steam haulage, resulting in his steam rack locomotive being used in 1812.

From these beginnings railways were developed for both freight and passengers. The first of the new railways to reach Leeds, with a terminal at Marsh Lane, was the Leeds & Selby Railway in 1834, nine years after the world's first public steam railway, built by George Stephenson between Darlington and Stockton.

The next major route to open was the North Midland Railway from Derby to Leeds Hunslet Lane in 1840, which reached the city via Normanton; this route was also linked to other lines to enable through trains to run between York and Leeds via Castleford and the first trans-Pennine trains from Manchester to Leeds via the Calder Valley and Normanton. Trains began running between Bradford and Leeds via Shipley in 1846 to a new Wellington station, which was the first in the city centre. This was followed by the opening of Leeds Central station in 1848, initially the terminus for Manchester trains, followed in 1849 by trains from Harrogate and the North. The shorter route between Bradford and Leeds via Stanningley opened in 1854.

The Great Northern Railway had since 1847 been running its express trains between London and Leeds via Knottingley and Methley, but was seeking a direct route into Leeds, which it achieved in 1857 by the opening of the line via Ardsley, then 1869 saw the completion of a major project to link the North Eastern at Marsh Lane with the London & North Western Railway at Holbeck, thus creating the first cross-city rail route as well as the opening of Leeds New station.

A summary of lines opened between 1834 and 1870 is shown in the table overleaf, which shows the pioneering early railway companies and their progressive evolution into today's privatised companies that operate current rail services in the Leeds area. During this time the basic railway network of Leeds was nearing completion. Most of the main centres of population had been linked, but the railways continued to develop with new lines continuing to be opened, and the widening of lines to accommodate growing rail traffic.

Mathew Murray's steam-powered rack locomotive and coal trucks on the Middleton Railway, 1812.

The first Leeds passenger railway: the Leeds & Selby Railway, 1834.

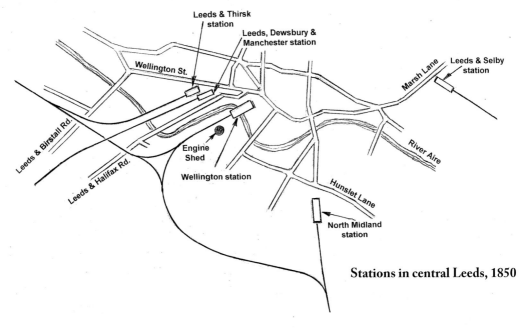

Stations in central Leeds, 1850

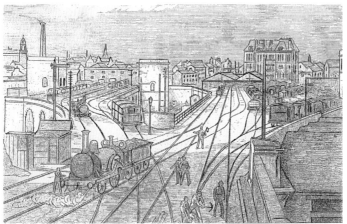

A lithograph that appeared in the *Illustrated London News* in 1868 showing Leeds Central station viewed from Holbeck Junction. The two-span roof can be seen in the distance; this was later extended to three, after which it remained virtually unchanged until its closure in 1967.

An early GNR train at Batley station. Although just over the present Leeds boundary, this train would have been bound for either Bradford via Drighlington or Leeds via Tingley, and is hauled by a Stirling 2-4-0 locomotive. The extensive station facilities reflect the confidence of the railway era. *Morley History Society*

Railways built to serve Leeds between 1834 and 1870, and their subsequent ownership

1834-1922		1923 Grouping	1948 Nationalisation	Privatisation
Leeds & Selby (LSR) York & North Midland (YNMR) Leeds & Thirsk (LTR)	North Eastern Railway (NER)	London & North Eastern (LNER)	British Railways	East Coast
Leeds Bradford & Halifax Junction (LBHJR) West Yorkshire (WYR)	Great Northern (GNR)			Cross Country
East & West Yorkshire Union (EWYUR)	Great Central			
North Midland (NMR) Leeds & Bradford (LBR)	Midland (MR)	London, Midland & Scottish (LMS)		North East Regional
Leeds, Dewsbury & Manchester (LDMR)	London & North Western (LNWR)			Midland Mainline
Manchester & Leeds (MLR)	Lancashire & Yorkshire (LYR)			Trans-Pennine Express
Track authorities: Railtrack (1994-2002), Network Rail (2002-)				

Opening dates of passenger lines and stations 1834-70

Date	Company	Service	Stations
1834	LSR	Marsh Lane-Selby	Marsh Lane, Osmondthorpe (op 1930), Cross Gates, Garforth, Micklefield
1840	NMR	Hunslet Lane-Normanton	Hunslet Lane, Hunslet (op 1854), Woodlesford, Methley North
1846	LBR	Leeds Wellington-Bradford Market Street	Armley (op 1847), Kirkstall, Kirkstall Forge (op 1860), Newlay, Calverley
1848	YNMR	Church Fenton-Harrogate	Thorpe Arch, Wetherby (station later relocated on Leeds line), Wetherby Racecourse (op 1924)
	LDMR	Leeds Central-Dewsbury	Wortley, Churwell, Morley Low
1849	LTR	Leeds Central-Harrogate	Holbeck (op 1855), Headingley, Horsforth, Arthington
	LYR	Methley Junction-Pontefract	Methley (LYR)
1854	LBHJR	Leeds Central-Bradford Adolphus Street	Holbeck, Armley & Wortley, Bramley, Stanningley
1856	LBHJR	Gildersome-Bradford	Gildersome, Drighlington & Adwalton
1857	WYR	Leeds Central-Wakefield Westgate	Beeston (op 1860), Ardsley
	LBHJR	Ardsley-Gildersome	Tingley (op 1858), Morley Top
1864	LBHJR	Adwalton Junction-Batley	
1865	NER	Arthington-Otley	Pool, Otley
	MR	Apperley Junction-Otley/Ilkley	Guiseley
1869	NER	Marsh Lane-Holbeck	
	Lofthouse-Methley	Methley South (Joint station)	

2
Arrival of the tramways

It is believed that a road coach began to run between Bramley and Leeds as early as 1833, and was followed by others with the result that a network of stagecoach services became established.

The first horse tramway to open in the city was from Boar Lane to Headingley, on 16 September 1871. This was a standard gauge line operated by the Leeds Tramway Company with a lease from the Council. Over the next few years other routes were opened, to Kirkstall in 1872, and Hunslet, Chapeltown and Marsh Lane in 1874.

By 1877 Kitson & Co was experimenting with steam trams, first using a tramcar with a vertical boiler but later changing to a locomotive-type tram with trailer car for passengers. Regular steam-operated services began from 1880, which stimulated further new tramways to be built in the densely populated city areas. Thomas Green also constructed steam tram locomotives for Leeds, and in all 68 trailer cars were used.

Leeds Corporation took over the trams in 1894 with the idea of using electricity. After earlier trials in 1891, electric traction was introduced between Kirkstall and Roundhay in 1897. Greenwood & Batley won a contract to supply some of the first electric tramcars for Leeds, and by 1900 there were 75 in operation, and all the horse and steam routes were electrified by 1902. The last horse tram route from City Square to Whitehall Road closed in 1901, and the last steam tram ran on the Stanningley route in 1902.

With all the former horse and steam tramways now converted to electric operation, attention was turned to extending to new areas. Surrounding towns were now looking to introduce electric tramways. In 1904 the Leeds system was linked up to lines running to Rothwell and Wakefield. Trams ran to Pudsey in 1908, Guiseley in 1909 and Morley in 1911.

A notable event occurred in 1907 when through running of trams commenced between Leeds and Bradford. The track gauge of the Bradford trams was 4 feet, as against

This undated view shows a horse-drawn tram with three horses in an unidentified area of Leeds. This form of transport began operation in Leeds from 1871 and gave great improvements compared to that previously provided over poor roads. Advertisements for Milkmaid Milk and EVO Whisky can be seen. *Reproduced by permission of Leeds Library & Information Services*

the standard-gauge (4ft 8½in) trams of Leeds. The result was the first dual-gauge tramcars in the world, which had special trucks with wheels arranged to slide over fixed axles. The wheels were locked in position for normal running but were released and allowed to adjust themselves to the other gauge by running over a short length of taper track connecting the two systems. This change of gauge took place at Stanningley.

The sequence of openings of the various tramways during the period 1871 to 1929 is shown in the table overleaf. However, the Whitehall Road tramway, from City Square to Whitehall Road (Cattle Market), was closed down in 1922 and was later to become part of the Farnley electric trackless route.

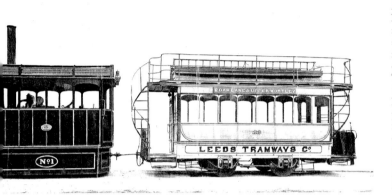

Left: **Horse-drawn trams required large numbers of horses and much manpower, and after the success of steam on the railways the tramways introduced steam to streetcar operations. Here is a Leeds Tramways Company steam tram in 1880, with Kitson steam tram No 1 hauling a Starbuck horse car. This particular tram locomotive was first used for a passenger service on 17 June 1880 and completed the journey between Boar Lane and Upper Wortley in 20 minutes.** *Reproduced by permission of Leeds Library & Information Services*

Below: **By 1902 all Leeds trams were electric. They were initially four-wheeled vehicles but later tramcars were developed with bogies, which gave a smoother ride. Despite this, four-wheeled trams survived until the end of tramway operation. Here No 351 is shown in City Square in 1939 on the 27 service to Cardigan Road.** *Leeds Transport Historical Society*

Leeds tramways, 1871-1929	
Opening date	Route
1871	Horse-drawn tramway, Boar Lane-Headingley
1872-79	Horse-drawn tramways, Leeds to Chapeltown, Kirkstall Road, Hunslet, Marsh Lane, Meanwood and Wortley
1880	Introduction of steam trams to Wortley after earlier trials
1890	Horse-drawn service to Roundhay (Oakwood) commenced
1891	First electric service to Roundhay, and the first in Britain to use overhead wires
1897	First Corporation electric service from Roundhay to Kirkstall via city centre
1897-99	New tramway to Hyde Park via Woodhouse Street and extensions to New Inn and Whingate, Marsh Lane-York Road and to Beckett Street and Victoria Road
1900	New tramways to Dewsbury Road, Beeston, Elland Road and Armley
1901	Aire Street-Whitehall Road (Cattle Market) and city to Cardigan Road via Burley Road
1902	Tramways extended from Armley to Bramley/Stanningley; completion of loop, Chapeltown to Roundhay Park
1904-05	New branches to Domestic Street and Compton Road; extended tramways from Hunslet to Rothwell/Wakefield, Swan Junction-Balm Road and York Road-Halton Dial
1906	Extensions, Kirkstall-Horsforth and Bramley-Rodley
1907	Stanningley-Bradford (Bradford Tramways) with through Leeds-Bradford service
1908	Stanningley-Pudsey, South Accommodation Road branch
1909	Horsforth-Guiseley
1911	Elland Road-Morley (-Bruntcliffe/Tingley Mills in 1912)
1913	Tramway extension to Lawnswood
1915	Halton Dial-Halton
1916	Halton Dial-Killingbeck
1924	Killingbeck-Cross Gates, Halton-Temple Newsam
1925	Dewsbury Road-Middleton (Middleton Light Railway)

The first tram to reach Morley, No 237, passes through Morley Bottoms in 1911 on its return journey to Leeds. This was one of the ten new tramcars specially bought by Leeds Corporation to operate the new route. *Morley History Society*

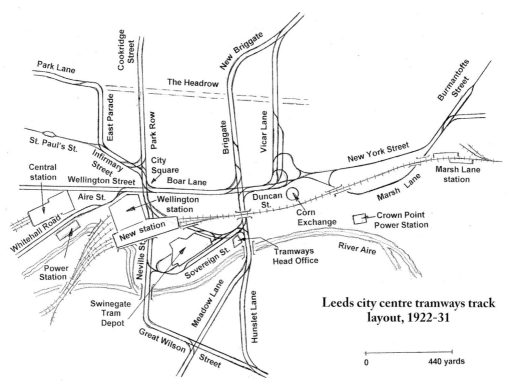

Leeds city centre tramways track layout, 1922-31

The Middleton Light Railway was opened in 1925 and ran from Dewsbury Road through Middleton Woods to a terminus at Middleton to serve the new housing estates of south Leeds. This 1953 picture shows 'Middleton Bogie' car No 255 bound for Middleton on Circular route 12 passing through the picturesque Middleton Woods on a snowy day. There was a tram stop in the middle of the woods where passengers could join or alight. *Leeds Transport Historical Society*

Leeds City Tramway route numbers

Route No	Later No(s)	Route	Route No	Later No(s)	Route
1		Lawnswood	16	15 & 16	Whingate, New Inn
2*		Moortown	17		Harehills Lane
			17	20	Halton
3*		Roundhay	18		Cross Gates
4		Kirkstall, Guiseley	19		Lower Wortley
5		Beeston	20		Accommodation Road
6		Woodhouse Street	21	11	Gipton
7		Belle Vue Road	22		Temple Newsam
8		Elland Road	23	6	Meanwood
9		Dewsbury Road	24	8	Elland Road, Morley
10		Compton Road	25		Hunslet, Rothwell
11		Harehills Road, Roundhay via Beckett St	26		Balm Road
			27	26*	Belle Isle
12*		Middleton	27		Cardigan Road
14		Pudsey, Half Mile Lane	29		Domestic Street
15		Rodley	30		Victoria Road

Routes were originally numbered in 1926 but were renumbered in 1929; this table is based on the latter together with subsequent amendments.

* These were also circular routes.

Abandoned tramway routes in Leeds, 1932 to 1945

Closure date	Route No	Route	Closure date	Route No	Route
1932	25	Hunslet-Rothwell	1936	17	Selby Road-Halton Village
1932	WR	Hunslet-Wakefield	1936	30	East Parade-Victoria Road
1934	7	Meanwood Road-Hyde Park-Park Lane	1937	29	Lane End Place-Domestic Street Terminus
1934	4	Hawksworth Road-Guiseley	1938	15	Bramley Town End-Rodley
1935	24	Churwell Dye Works-Morley, Bruntcliffe and Tingley	1938	14	Cohens Foundry-Stanningley Bottom-Pudsey Terminus
1936	20	South Accommodation Road-York Road	1938	24	Churwell Dye Works-Elland Road

The tramway branch to Gipton opened in 1936 and was intended as part of a route to Seacroft. The Council obtained a Light Railway Order in 1939 authorising the extension to Seacroft, and it was renewed during the war. Additionally Seacroft was included on tram destination blinds. However, despite this the project never materialised, nor did three other post-war attempts to serve Seacroft with rail transport. Here 'Horsfield' car No 172 is seen in Gipton cutting with a service for Dewsbury Road.
Dewi Williams

3
Development of the railway network

The growth of the railways continued into the last part of the 19th century with new lines opened and existing routes widened to give extra capacity.

A further line from Cross Gates to Wetherby opened in 1876, followed two years later by a route between Garforth and Castleford and the Pudsey loop line. Two large projects were to follow with the Beeston to Batley line in 1890 and the Leeds New line in 1900. Both these routes involved major engineering work with flyovers at the Leeds end to give ample future capacity.

In 1904 The East & West Yorkshire Union Railway introduced a Leeds Wellington to Robin Hood passenger service. Unfortunately this could not compete with the tramways and was short-lived, being withdrawn after only nine months. This was one of the few casualties of tramway competition, which was certainly felt but consisted mainly of the railways having to cut their fares and run shorter trains on some routes. The railway companies also objected to some Tramway Bills to construct new competitive routes.

A summary of the opening of passenger railways between 1871 to 1904 is given in the accompanying table.

The stations at Stourton, Rothwell and Robin Hood closed in 1904, and Kirkstall Forge in 1905, but otherwise the railways continued to grow, with heavier and longer main-line passenger trains, up to the First World War. After war service the railways were run-down, and major changes were on the horizon. In 1923 the many individual railway companies were 'grouped' into four larger concerns. Two of these, the LMS and LNER, would run rail services in the Leeds area until nationalisation in 1948.

In the inter-war years and during the Second World War a number of stations serving sparsely populated villages were closed, at Gildersome (St Bernards) in 1921, Woodkirk in 1939, Churwell in 1940 and Methley (LYR) in 1943. Although the official closure date for Churwell is 1940, from local sources it is believed that it closed some time earlier in 1939. During the same period a number of new stations were built, mainly to serve new Leeds Corporation housing estates at Osmondthorpe in 1930 and Penda's Way in 1939. The latter was reported as having been built in a day on previously prepared foundations. A halt at Bower on the Garforth to Castleford line opened in 1934.

Another aspect of the arrival of the railways had a major impact on the British way of life – local times had to be unified, allowing timetables to be introduced. All railway stations would have a clock, and staff were issued with pocket watches. Bradshaw published his first national railway *Guide* in 1838. Timekeeping thus became, and has always been, very important to the railways.

Opening dates of passenger lines and stations, 1871-1904			
Date		Service	Stations
1876	NER	Cross Gates-Wetherby	Penda's Way (op 1939), Scholes, Thorner, Bardsey, Collingham Bridge, Wetherby
1878	NER	Garforth-Castleford	Kippax, Bower (op 1934), Ledston
	GNR	Pudsey Loop	Pudsey Lowtown, Pudsey Greenside
1890	GNR	Beeston Junction-Batley	Woodkirk
1900	LNWR	Farnley Junction-Spen Valley	Gildersome LNWR (Leeds New line)
1904	EWYUR	Stourton Junction-Robin Hood	Stourton, Rothwell, Robin Hood

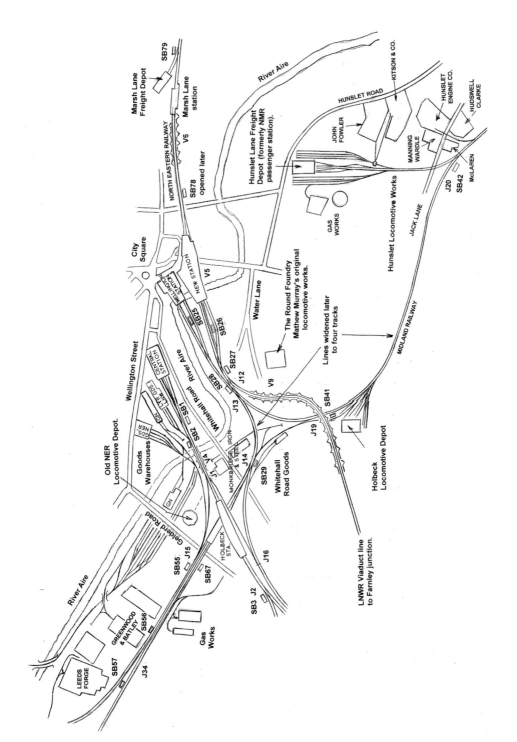

Central Leeds station, depots and sidings.

For the names of the junctions, signal boxes and viaducts coded 'J', 'SB' and 'V', see pages 97, 98 and 101 respectively.

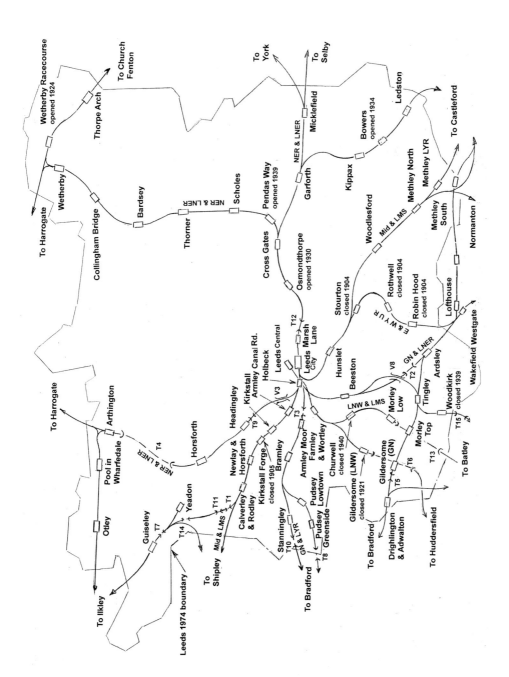

Passenger railways of Leeds, 1902–48.

For the names of the tunnels and viaducts coded 'T' and 'V', see page 101.

4
Tramways, 1930-59

After the First World War the omnibus was starting to appear and, with improved roads being provided, it became a competitor to the tramways on some routes. The tram was being affected on two fronts: on its routes to sparsely populated outlying towns, and with a shift in population from densely populated inner-city areas to new housing estates further out. As a result, in the inter-war period the trams to Guiseley, Morley, Pudsey and Rothwell were abandoned, as were those to Bradford and Wakefield. Additionally, short routes to Victoria Road and Domestic Street also finished. This left the tramways running on the densely populated trunk routes and their financial performance improved with the trams carrying large numbers of people at cheap fares, which remained unaltered between 1928 and 1944. This policy was very successful and in 1939 the system carried around 200 million passengers annually on 52 route miles of track.

After the First World War a tramway parcel service was set up, which proved to be very successful. In 1930 the Parcel Department of Leeds Tramways had a staff of 69.

Leeds also pioneered an improved design of tramcar to improve passenger comfort. From 1933 a new kind of bogie tram for the Middleton route was introduced. In 1937 the last new tram depot was opened at Torre Road; earlier depots that served the Leeds tramway system over 85 years of operation were at Bramley (1905-1949); Burmantofts (1891-1939); Chapeltown (1876-1939); Guiseley (1915-1934); Headingley (1874-1954); Hunslet (1875-1940); Kirkstall Road (1897-1931; also a tramway engineering works until 1957); Morley (1920-1935); Rothwell (1904-1932; West Riding Tramways depot); and Swinegate (1915-1959) Torre Road closed in 1955.

Some new tramways and extensions continued up to 1949 on routes to serve new housing estates in east and south Leeds, despite trams being abandoned in some other parts of the city. The branch from York Road to Gipton, opened in 1936, was intended to eventually form a new tram route to Seacroft. Other extensions were from Balm Road to Belle Isle (1940) and Belle Isle to Middleton (1949).

Leeds found that it was cheaper to lay track on reserved strips rather than along city streets. As a result a policy of providing reserved track was adopted. The Harehills to Roundhay route was the first in 1923, followed by others, and the Middleton Light Railway through Middleton Woods was opened in 1925. Even on roads served by buses space was left for future tramways should the demand develop.

During the Second World War the trams served the city well, but at its end the system and the tramcars were very run-down and as a result second-hand tramcars were bought; former Hull, London, Manchester and Southampton trams operated over the Leeds system.

Despite some routes being closed, plans were still being made for a future modernised tramway network. In 1945 a plan was drawn up for city centre subways (see Chapter 14), followed by proposals for a change to railcars, of which three single-deck examples were built.

However, in the end it became a choice between development or abandonment, and unfortunately road transport interests, which wanted to see the end of the tramways, won the day. As a result a decision was taken by the Labour-controlled Leeds City Council to abandon the tramway system, and the last trams ran on 7 November 1959.

Above: The trams soon became used for moving large crowds at the football grounds of Elland Road, Headingley and Parkside. Also large numbers of people were moved to the beauty spots of Roundhay Park, Temple Newsam and Kirkstall Abbey. Here trams are lining up outside the Elland Road ground in Low Fields Road awaiting the end of a Leeds United match, after which they will swiftly move large numbers of people with great efficiency. *Leeds Transport Historical Society*

Below: Passengers board Chamberlain car No 122 in Commercial Road, Kirkstall. Opponents of the tramways always quoted the difficulty of street loading as an argument for their abolition. Supporters, however, argued for the tramways to be converted to modern operation by being segregated from other traffic. *Leeds Transport Historical Society*

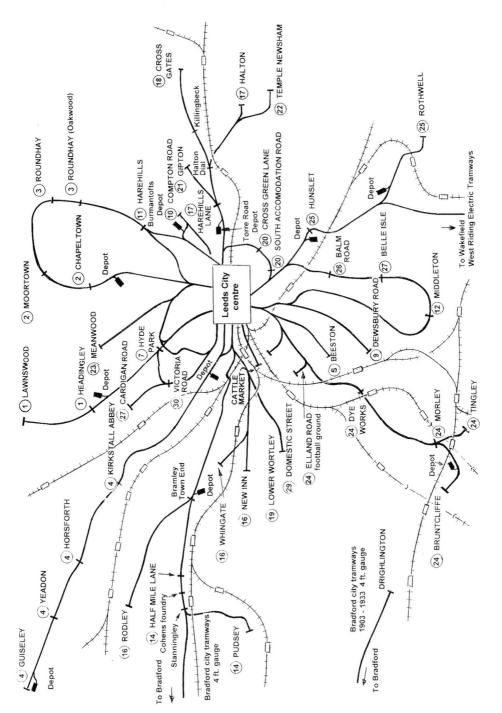

Leeds City Tramways, 1871 - 1959

Post-war plans were to put the tramways on reserved tracks to segregate them from other traffic. Here Horsfield car No 164 stands at a tram stop on the segregated tramway in Stanningley Road in 1952, with a route 14 service for Half Mile Lane. *Dewi Williams*

The post-Second World War Leeds City Transport tramway fleet					
Leeds-built trams					
LCT Nos	Type	Date built	LCT Nos	Type	Date built
1-150	Chamberlain	1925-28	321, 332, 339-341, 343-369	Converts from open cars	1921-22
151-245	Horsfield	1930-31	370-393, 399-402	Beeston air-braked	1923-25
255-274	Middleton bogies	1933-35	394-398, 400-445	Chamberlain	1925-28
275, 276*	Converts	1921-22	601, 602	Railcars	1953
* Numbers taken in 1943/1948 for new-build cars					
Trams bought second-hand					
LCT Nos	From	Date bought	Date built		
277-279/301	London	1939/1951	1930/1932		
280-286	Manchester	1946	1925-31		
290-300	Southampton	1949	1930		
446-487	Hull	1942-45	1904-11		
501-590	London (Feltham class)	1949	1931		
600	Sunderland	1944	Rebuilt 1953		

Leeds acquired a large number of second-hand trams for the post-year period. The best and most numerous of these were the large ex-London Feltham bogie tramcars, of which 90 were bought. Car No 527 is shown at the rural terminus of Temple Newsam in 1952. *Dewi Williams*

Personal tramway reminiscences

Although living at Gildersome I used the Leeds trams extensively and found them to be a superb form of urban transport that never let me down. My grandparents had the Swan with Two Necks public house in Hunslet, which was at Swan Junction with the tram tracks running on either side so we could reach it by catching either a Hunslet, Middleton or Belle Isle tram. Following my grandfather's death, my grandmother moved to Roundhay Road, so then the No 3 tram was used. A further move was to Middleton which involved the best tram journey of all via the Middleton Railway, Parkside, then through Middleton Woods. An alternative was to travel round the circle via Belle Isle.

My other grandparents lived at Osmondthorpe, which involved using the Cross Gates or Halton trams. In addition there were visits to Roundhay Park, Temple Newsam and Headingley, for example, where trams moved vast numbers of people with the greatest of efficiency.

Without doubt Leeds had one of the finest tramways in the country, but it became clear that after years of neglect it needed major modernisation. It was very reassuring when in 1953 the new single-decker tramcars arrived in a new purple livery to celebrate the Queen's Coronation. They were modern and comfortable and were to give the trams a golden future. However, regrettably, as with so many other Leeds transport projects, it was a false dawn.

Above right: **Two single-deck tramcars, Nos 601 and 602, were built together with the converted ex-Sunderland car No 600 as prototypes for future subway and reserved-track operation with trailers. Here we see car No 601 bound for Corn Exchange at the Chapeltown terminus at Stainbeck Lane in 1953. Because of their limited capacity of 34 seats, 36 standing, the single railcars were used mostly on the short Hunslet service.** *Leeds Transport Historical Society*

Right: **My grandparents' public house, The Swan with Two Necks, was located at the junction of Hunslet Road and Whitfield Road. This became known as Swan Junction, with the trams running to Hunslet on the left and Belle Isle on the right. The picture was taken in 1974 when the pub was boarded up ready for demolition. A Leeds City Transport No 7 bus bound for Leeds is passing; this was the replacement service for the No 25 Hunslet tramway service, but the buses never achieved the quality of service or affection that people had for the trams.** *Author*

Abandoned tramway routes, 1946-1959		
Closure date	Route No	Route
1946	19	Lower Wortley Terminus-Oldfield Lane
	11	Beckett Street-Harehills Road
1947	4	St Paul's Street-West Street Cardigan Road-Victoria Road
1949	4	Hawksworth Road-Kirkstall Abbey
1953	14	Cohens Foundry-Half Mile Lane-Wellington Road
1954	4	Kirkstall Abbey-Wellington Street
	10	Compton Road-York Road
1955	11	Gipton-York Road
	6	Meanwood-Sheepscar
	8	Elland Road-Meadow Road
	5	Beeston-Meadow Road
1956	1	Lawnswood-City Square
	15/16	Whingate/New Inn-Briggate
1957	2	Moortown-Chapeltown-Sheepscar
	9	Dewsbury Road-Moor Road
1959	12/26/27	Middleton-Belle Isle-Meadow Lane
	3	Moortown-Roundhay-Briggate
	25	Hunslet-Briggate
	17/18/20/22	Temple Newsam/Halton/Cross Gates/Harehills Lane-Briggate

LEEDS CITY TRANSPORT DEPARTMENT

CROSS GATES, HALTON & TEMPLE NEWSAM TRAM SERVICES

THIS TICKET WAS ISSUED ON THE LAST DAY OF OPERATION, SATURDAY NOVEMBER 7th 1959, TO MARK THE CLOSING DOWN OF THE TRAMWAY SYSTEM IN LEEDS.

Fare 2d.

19003

The special ticket issued for the last day of Leeds tramway operation.

Tramcar operation in the City of Leeds commenced in 1871. The first line was opened for traffic with horse trams between Boar Lane and the Oak Inn, Headingley on 16th September.
Steam trams were introduced on the Wortley route on 17th June, 1880 and electric trams on the Roundhay route on 11th November, 1891.
For 10 years three different forms of traction were in operation but the last horse trams ran on 13th October, 1901 and the last steam trams on 1st April, 1902.
From the beginning of the century the electric tramway system grew rapidly as various extensions were made. The era of the electric tram reached its peak in 1933 when the fleet totalled 476 trams running over 124 miles of track.

Large crowds turned out for the last day of the Leeds trams on 7 November 1959. Here Horsfield car No 187 stands at Cross Gates terminus in the afternoon gloom of the final day of tramway operation. *Leeds Transport Historical Society*

5
Post-war railway changes

The railways were also in a very run-down condition at the end of the Second World War and this led to nationalisation in 1948, when British Railways was born. Local services carried on very much as before with steam traction and little investment, but a small number of lightly used stations and branch lines were closed. These included Kippax, Bower and Ledston in 1951, Farnley & Wortley (1952), Beeston (1953), Tingley (1954), Gildersome GNR (1955), Methley North (1957), Holbeck and Marsh Lane (1958), Wetherby Racecourse (1959), Hunslet, Osmondthorpe and Methley South (1960), Morley Top (1961), and Drighlington (1962).

In 1954, however, a determined effort was made to modernise services when diesel multiple units (DMUs) began to be introduced on the more important lines to replace steam trains. These greatly increased the patronage of local trains but unfortunately came at a time when the national Government was seeking to close down as much of the railway system as possible in a bid to make the railways pay.

Ex-GNR Class 'C1' 4-4-2 No 3274 is at the head of a Pullman train at Leeds Central in the 1930s. These outstanding locomotives, designed by H. A. Ivatt, were the forerunners of the Gresley 'Pacifics'. They were fitted with a massive boiler with Wootten firebox, which formed the basis of the later 4-6-2 engines. *M. Bentley*

Above: Experimental LNER 4-6-4 No 10000 is seen at Leeds in 1931. This engine, designed by Nigel Gresley in 1929, had a Yarrow water tube boiler, but was rebuilt with a conventional boiler in 1937. *M. Bentley*

Below: A fine study of unnamed LMS 'Patriot' Class 4-6-0 No 5550 at Holbeck shed in 1934. These locomotives were introduced in 1930 by Fowler and later rebuilt with taper boilers. *M. Bentley*

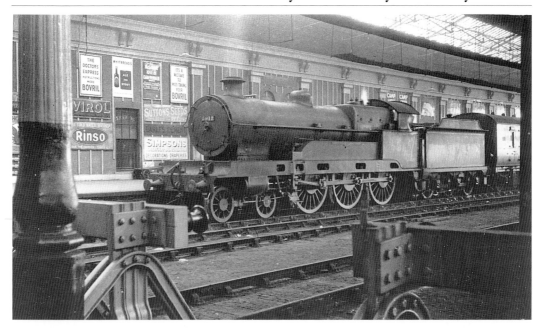

Above: Until the arrival of the Stanier express engines the most powerful LMS locomotives were the ex-LNWR 4-6-0 types. Here 'Claughton' No 5912 *Lord Faber* stands at Leeds station buffer stops after arrival with an express in 1935. *Stephenson Locomotive Society*

Right: A Class 'B1' 4-6-0 with a Leeds to Hull express passes Osmondthorpe in 1959. This four-track section ran from Marsh Lane to the Wetherby line junction at Cross Gates, giving ample line capacity, and was very heavily used by all types of rail traffic. *Author*

Below: Following nationalisation British Railways built numerous ex-LMS designs of locomotive, which worked on both ex-LMS and ex-LNER routes. Here we see Class 5MT 2-6-0 No 43044 designed by H. G. Ivatt, son of H. A. Ivatt, at Stourton in 1965. These locomotives had quite an austere appearance but were tidied up to become the BR Standard Class 4 2-6-0. *Lens of Sutton Association*

The Beeching era

The Conservative Minister of Transport, Ernest Marples, who incidentally owned a road-building firm, appointed Richard Beeching as Chairman of British Railways and gave him the task of being the 'hatchet man'. His report, *The Reshaping of British Railways*, was published in 1963 and advocated the closing of 5,000 route miles of track and 2,362 passenger stations.

Leeds railway services were hit particularly hard by the closure proposals, which would have reduced the number of local stations to only six. Fortunately public opposition to the closures saved three stations from the axe.

Passenger services to be withdrawn were Doncaster-Leeds Central (local), Leeds Central-Castleford Central-Pontefract, Leeds City-Knottingley, Leeds Central-Pudsey-Bradford Exchange, Leeds City-Keighley (local), Leeds City-Ilkley, Leeds City-Cudworth-Sheffield (local), and Leeds City-Wetherby-Harrogate.

Passenger stations and halts to be closed (with dates of closure in brackets) were Ardsley (1964), Armley Canal Road (165), Armley Moor (1966), Bardsey (1964), Calverley & Rodley (1965), Collingham Bridge (1964), Guiseley (saved), Kirkstall (1965), Newlay (1965), Otley (1965), Thorner (1964), Penda's Way (1964), Pool in Wharfedale (1965), Pudsey Greenside (1964), Pudsey Lowtown (1964), Scholes (1964), Thorpe Arch (1964), Wetherby (1964) and Woodlesford (saved). Bramley and Morley Low were added later to the closure list; Bramley closed in 1966, but Morley Low was saved. Later Stanningley closed in 1968, and Leeds Whitehall (the temporary station opened in 1999 for the Leeds station rebuilding) in 2002.

Above right: **From the mid-1950s diesel traction began to replace steam. Here a Class 104 diesel multiple unit forms a Leeds to Hull train passing Peckfield Colliery in 1979. The closed colliery site has now been cleared and is being considered as a site for a new East Leeds parkway station.** *Author*

Right: **The Eastern Region of British Rail opened Britain's first parkway station at New Pudsey in 1968. The station was a replacement for Stanningley and built near the city outer ring road with extensive car parking facilities and served by inter-city trains. Shown here is a King's Cross to Bradford Exchange train stopping at the station in 1979. Since then all long-distance trains have been withdrawn and the station is now an ordinary suburban station.** *Author*

From 1965 British Railways revealed a new corporate image including a shortened operational name and the introduction of the 'double arrow' symbol, which was to be used on all trains, timetables and stations. With the privatisation of British Rail this symbol passed to the Department for Transport and continues to be used on maps and at stations to indicate the national rail network.

There was also to be rationalisation of parcel traffic, concentration of traffic on bulk loads, liner trains and container trains. Most wagonload freight was to be discouraged through small goods station closures and rate rises. Coaching and wagon stock were to be greatly reduced, and much stock for excursion trains was to be scrapped.

Against the trend New Pudsey station opened in 1967, but this was intended more as a motorist inter-city railhead station than for local travel. In 1967 the rebuilt Leeds City station was completed, and in 1966 British Railways issued the formal closure notice for Leeds Central station, which also included the discontinuance of the sections of line from Gelderd Junction to Three Signal Bridge Junction, Three Signal Bridge Junction to Leeds Central, Holbeck Junction to Three Signal Bridge Junction, and Farnley Junction to Bridge No 6 (Gelderd Road).

A fairly skeletal local railway network for Leeds had thus been saved, but economies continued to be made with some stations becoming unmanned, and fares being collected on the trains to replace the closed booking offices.

Despite the Beeching cuts British Railways failed to become profitable and the result was the 1968 Transport Act to reconstruct railway finances. A main element of the new Act was the provision of grants for uneconomic but socially necessary passenger services. These became payable from 1969 and all local services running into Leeds received them. For the first time for many years some stability was restored to local train services. Despite this Leeds transport policy was still very much biased towards road transport (see Chapter 13).

The West Yorkshire Passenger Transport Executive

A very important change came in 1974 with the reorganisation of local government. This created the new county of West Yorkshire, of which Leeds was the largest of five district councils. A major part of the new set-up was the formation of the West Yorkshire Passenger Transport Executive (WYPTE), charged with responsibility for the planning and integration of all passenger transport in the new county.

WYPTE brought new thinking to the region and saw an increased role for rail services. As a result services began to be improved, with more trains being run and the previous skeleton services first becoming hourly, then half-hourly on many routes. To achieve this more train units were ordered and the county pioneered new lightweight diesel units, the first being Class 141. Additionally new stations were opened by the new body: Bramley on 12 September 1983, East Garforth on 1 May 1987, Cottingley on 25 April 1988 and Burley Park on 28 November 1988.

Metro (WYPTE) carried out a new transportation study in 1977 and from this came a proposal to reopen a small spur using the old Castleford line to a new station at South Garforth. There was some public opposition to this and the scheme was dropped, but a station on the main line at East Garforth was later opened instead. A few years later a new East Leeds study was completed, and this came before the Passenger Transport Authority in 1989. It proposed relaying the four-track section to Cross Gates and reopening part of the Wetherby branch as far as Scholes. No action was taken at that time, but it remained an option for the future. Details of both schemes with possible station sites are shown on the accompanying map.

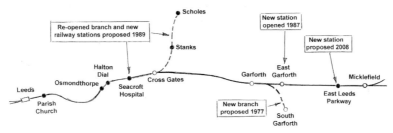

East Leeds rail proposals, 1977-2008

Right: A Class 307 electric multiple unit is parked in the bay platform at Leeds in 1990, between crew training duties. These units were acquired second-hand from the London area to operate the Leeds to Doncaster local service. The unit shown is still in Network SouthEast livery, before being painted in Metro crimson and cream. Later these were replaced by new Class 321 units. *Author*

Electrification

Electrification came to Leeds by way of a scheme to electrify the East Coast Main Line from London King's Cross to Leeds, Newcastle, Edinburgh and Glasgow. The first electric trains began running in August 1990 with a local Leeds to Doncaster service operated by second-hand Class 307 units from the London area. Later the WYPTE bought three new Class 321 units to run this service.

This scheme electrified the extensive Leeds City station layout, and on the back of this Metro carried out a local scheme to electrify the Leeds/Bradford to Ilkley/Skipton routes; electric trains began running in May 1995, again using old London area stock, but this time Class 308 units. Shortly afterwards Metro ordered 16 new three-car Class 333 trains to run the new services. A while later a fourth car was ordered, making the units into four-car trains to cope with rising patronage.

Privatisation

In 1993 Parliament passed the Railway Act, which privatised the nation's railways. From 1994 control passed from British Railways to new private companies. Railtrack became the track authority and a number of franchises were awarded to train operating companies. The uncertainty created by the new structure resulted in plans, then in the pipeline, to open new stations at Armley and the White Rose Centre being dropped.

However, in 1999 Metro carried out a further study to reopen Leeds stations, and the outcome was that stations at Kirkstall, Armley, Horsforth Ring Road and Ardsley met the criteria for opening. The Kirkstall and Horsforth locations were included in the first programme of proposed new stations.

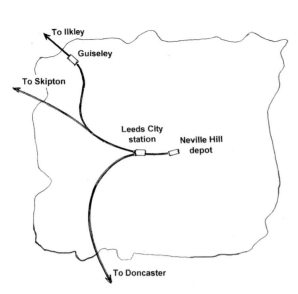

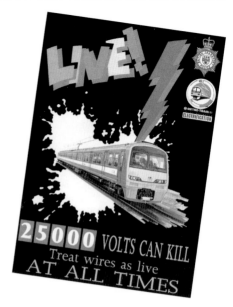

Above: **Electrification came late to the railways of Leeds. This is the extent of electric passenger services, 1990-95, serving only two Leeds stations.**

Above right: **This Railtrack railway safety leaflet, warning of the dangers from overhead electric wires, was issued for the introduction of the Airedale and Wharfedale electric services.**

Below: **The Class 91 electric locomotives, together with driving trailers for push-pull operation, were built by British Rail for the London to Leeds electrification. Here a Class 91 locomotive is seen after arrival at Leeds with a Great North Eastern Railway train from London King's Cross in 1997. GNER was one of the most successful and best-loved of the privatised companies and ran East Coast services for more than a decade from 1996.** *Author*

Above: For the Airedale and Wharfedale electrification redundant Class 308 EMU units from the London area were used to operate the service when it started in 1995. Later 18 new Class 333 units were built for the electric service. A new Class 333 unit is seen here at Leeds station in 2001. Due to the success of the electric trains extra coaches were ordered to convert them into four-car units to cater for the rapid growth in patronage. *Author*

Below: A Eurostar unit forms a train to London King's Cross at Leeds station in 2002. Four of these Channel Tunnel trains were leased by GNER to operate the 'White Rose' Leeds to London services. They were painted in the blue and red GNER livery, but occasionally a unit in Eurostar yellow livery would turn up, as shown here. A Class 321 unit on the right forms a local service to Doncaster. *Author*

Railtrack as a private company did not function satisfactorily, and in 2002 was replaced by Network Rail, a public 'not for profit' company. Once the privatised railway had settled down progress began to be made. The Leeds station rebuilding was completed in 2002 (see Chapter 10) and railway companies began to invest in new rolling stock and to increase the frequency of long-distance services. There were now four fast trains per hour between Leeds and Manchester, Virgin Trains introduced a new Leeds to Edinburgh service, and from 2007 GNER ran a half-hourly service between Leeds and London.

Northern Rail, together with Metro, also showed great initiative in improving regional services and, with conditions on the roads deteriorating due to congestion, rail travel into Leeds reached an all-time high. The only downside is that Leeds still has only a small number of suburban stations, although Metro still has plans to resume its programme of new station openings.

The number of passengers using train services has always been counted, usually through twice-yearly surveys, but the information was often sketchy. However, more information is now available. Basically, usage remained fairly steady until the 1950s, then plummeted after Beeching to subsequently recover and rise rapidly as transport policies changed and road congestion became worse. This trend is clearly shown in the accompanying graph.

We know that in 1958 2.25 million passengers used Leeds Central station annually, with another 2.75 million using City station, giving a combined total of 5 million. Today this has grown to more than 16 million passengers per year passing through the enlarged Leeds station. Similarly the number of users of West Yorkshire trains has risen from 14 million to almost 30 million over the same period. However, parcel and newspaper traffic is now non-existent, whereas in 1958 the two Leeds stations handled more than 3.25 million parcels, of which 1.25 million were for the Post Office.

Annual patronage of Leeds railway stations, 2007			
Station	No of passengers	Station	No of passengers
Leeds	16,059,517	Guiseley	730,110
Bramley	165,535	Headingley	222,649
Burley Park	426,489	Horsforth	729,780
Cottingley	43,504	Micklefield	138,050
Cross Gates	281,691	Morley	160,910
East Garforth	173,602	New Pudsey	489,095
Garforth	482,923	Woodlesford	196,723
		Total	4,241,061

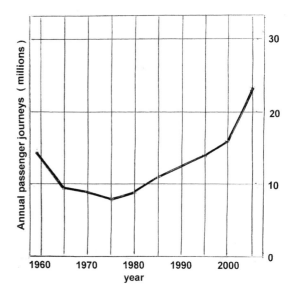

Above: **Patronage of West Yorkshire train services. The figures include all passengers on local trains together with local passengers within West Yorkshire on long-distance trains.**

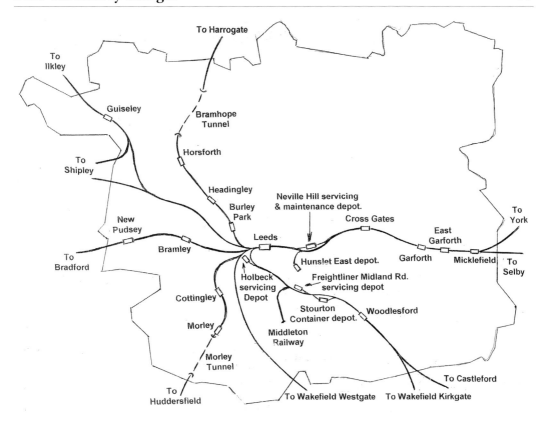

The railways of Leeds, 2009

Leeds station 2008: a view of the tallest building in Leeds (Bridgewater Place) seen between two units, one an ex-Central trains Class 158 and the other a Class 144, both in Platform 17. From 1990 Leeds saw rapid development as a financial centre with large-scale office building in the city centre generating a large increase in commuting. Unfortunately transport provision did not match, and existing rail services had to cope with a vast increase in passenger numbers leading to chronic overcrowding of trains. *Author*

6
Train services

Pre-First World War express services

Leeds to London services

1846: First through train service provided by the Midland Railway from Leeds Wellington to London Euston via Derby and Rugby, taking 7hr 40min for the 206 miles.

1851: GNR service via Askern and Lincoln in 5hr 45min, also for 206 miles.

1852: GNR route shortened to 186.5 miles with the opening of the direct route avoiding Lincoln.

1854: GNR uses Leeds Central, necessitating reversal out of the station to Gelderd Junction to access the MR/LYR route via Woodlesford and Askern.

1857: GNR route via Wakefield Westgate opened, trains routed via Kirkgate and Askern.

1868: MR line to London St Pancras opened, shortening the Midland route to 198 miles with a 5-hour journey time.

1869: Direct Wakefield-Doncaster line opened, enabling GNR trains to avoid running via Askern.

1874: MR introduces the first Pullman cars in Britain on St Pancras to Leeds and Bradford services; the new standard of comfort gives impetus to replacement of four- and six-wheeled coaches with bogie stock.

1880: GNR introduces first dining cars in the country on Leeds to London services.

1893: The short-lived GCR London Marylebone to Leeds Central service is withdrawn; it covered the 203 miles in 4hr 20min.

1901: Competition for the Leeds-London traffic by the MR and GNR – GNR takes 3hr 49min, MR 4hr 10min (later 3hr 50min by Scotch expresses).

Trans-Pennine services

The LYR ran express trains between Liverpool and Leeds Central via the Calder Valley. The NER and LNWR ran services from Liverpool and Manchester to Newcastle and Hull using rolling stock of both companies. Locomotives were normally changed at Leeds, although some LNWR locomotives ran through to Hull.

Scottish destinations

The MR and NER competed for the Scotch traffic with the MR running via Carlisle and the NER by way of Newcastle.

South West destinations

The MR ran trains to Bristol and the South West via Birmingham. The LNWR provided a service to South West destinations via Stockport.

Local stopping train services, 1922

The table on page 38 shows typical departures of local services from Leeds on Mondays to Fridays in 1922. Most trains stopped at all local stations on the route, although some lightly used stations had less frequent trains. As a comparison, the number of trains on the same lines in 1969 and 2008 are also shown, and the decline then startling increase in frequency is apparent, although these currently serve fewer Leeds suburban stations.

Above: **A Great Northern Railway local train bound for Wakefield and photographed from the viaduct climbs towards Tingley before entering Ardsley Tunnel. The train consists of a van and four non-bogie coaches and is hauled by a 4-4-0 locomotive.** *Morley History Society*

Right: **A local North Eastern Railway train hauled by an 0-4-4 tank engine calls at Cross Gates station. The NER ran a regular suburban service on its two main lines into Leeds, both of which survive today. The four tracks enabled express trains to pass at speed on the centre lines.** *Lens of Sutton Association*

Right: **The Lancashire & Yorkshire Railway ran an express service from Liverpool & Manchester into Leeds Central and also local trains from Leeds Wellington to Pontefract via Methley. It originally had a small engine shed at Copley Hill, but later served Leeds from Low Moor. Here LYR 4-4-0 No 996 is pictured at Leeds Central. The company was taken over by the LNWR in 1921 prior to the Grouping of 1923.** *LCGB, Ken Nunn collection*

Departures of local stopping trains from central Leeds stations, 1922			
	No of trains		
	1922	1969	2008
Airedale & Wharfedale lines, Leeds Wellington-Shipley/Otley (O)/Ilkley (I) – MR			
5.48, 6.34(O), 6.58, 8.02, 8.22, 9.08(I), 9.23, 11.00. 12.12, 13.08(I), 13.15, 14.02, 16.18, 16.26(I), 17.10, 17,43, 18.17, 19.30(I), 20.40, 21.45, 22.57	21	21*	95*
Calderdale line, Leeds Central-Bradford, direct and via Pudsey (P) – GNR			
5.15, 6.02(P), 6.20, 7.12, 8.00, 8.18(P), 9.25(P), 10.30(P), 12.05, 12.30(P), 13.05, 13.22(P), 14.25, 15.00(P), 16.00, 16.43(P), 17.11(P), 17.18, 17.46(P), 18.15, 18.45, 19.20(P), 20.10, 21.00, 21.55(P)	26	32	65
Hallam and Pontefract line, Leeds Wellington-Normanton (N)/Barnsley (B)/Sheffield (S) – MR; Leeds Wellington-Castleford Cutsyke-Pontefract (P) – LNWR, LYR until 1921			
6.30(S), 8.30(S), 8.58(P), 10.55(P), 12.08(B), 13.23(P), 15.50(P), 16.28(N), 17.32(P), 18.13(N), 20.00(P), 20.38(S), 21.10(N), 22.27(N)	14	23	34
Harrogate line, Leeds New-Arthington-Ilkley (I) – NER			
5.30, 7.53, 9.25 (I), 9.56, 11.50 (I), 12.56, 14.25, 14.53 (I), 16.20, 17.04 (I), 17.32 (I), 17.38, 18.05, 19.05, 21.00 (I), 21.48	16	17	35
Huddersfield line, Leeds New-Huddersfield – LNWR			
5.50, 6.25, 7.20, 8.10, 9.30, 10.00, 11.25, 12.15, 13.25, 14.47, 16.10, 16.55, 17.42, 18.55, 20.00, 21.30, 23.05	17	8	31
Micklefield line, Leeds New-Castleford (C)/Selby (S)/Wetherby (W)/York (Y) – NER			
5.30(S), 6.30(W), 6.38(Y), 6.48(C), 7.55(W), 8.12(C), 9.45(W), 10.17(Y), 12.05(C), 12.24(S), 13.08, 13.28(W), 14.42(S), 15.05(C), 15.25(Y), 16.16(W), 17.06(S), 17.30(W), 17.52(Y), 18.08(C), 18.45(W), 19.00(S), 20.03(Y), 21.05(Y), 20.27(W), 21.55(W), 22.10(S)	27	26	33
Wakefield line, Leeds Central-Castleford (C)/Wakefield (W)/Batley via Tingley (B)/ Drighlington via Tingley (D) – GNR			
5.07(B), 5.20(C), 6.06(B), 7.08(W), 7.56, 8.43(W), 8.52(C), 9.10(B), 9.28(W), 11.40(W), 11.55(B), 12.18(D), 12.08(C), 14.00(W), 14.10(D), 14.50(B), 15.25(W), 16.20(C), 16.25(D), 16.46(W), 17.23(D), 17.55(W), 17.38(D), 18.18(C), 18.35(D), 19.26(W), 20.05(D), 20.33(B), 21.15(W). 21.52(D), 22.23(W), 22.28(D)	32	6*	35*
No stations served in Leeds (except Guiseley)			

Local Leeds
pre-Grouping
train services

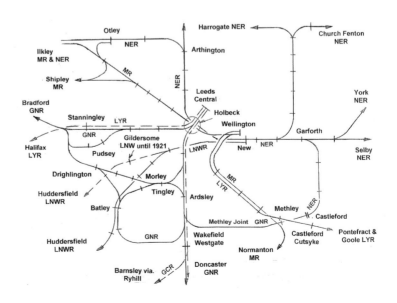

Inter-city and long-distance services

Leeds has always had good rail links to most parts of the country. The duplication of routes that existed in the old days of the private companies was eliminated after nationalisation and BR started the development of the remaining trunk routes, which has been continued by the new franchised railway operating companies. The table below provides a comparison of the number of trains and journey times over the last century for rail travel between Leeds and Britain's major cities.

In the golden age of rail travel in the first half of the 20th century a number of crack trains operated and these usually carried names such as the 'West Riding' and the 'Thames-Clyde Express'. In addition, Pullman trains were run with more luxurious carriages, for which passengers paid a supplementary charge on top of the normal fare. As the speed and frequency of train services increased these became less significant and train names were gradually phased out. Named trains that served Leeds are shown in the table overleaf.

Leeds-London in 175 minutes

On November 16th 1933 a record run was recorded with the up 'Queen of Scots' Pullman. Leaving Leeds 18 minutes late and with some swift running, it arrived in King's Cross dead on time, covering the 185.8 miles in 2 hours and 55 minutes, giving an overall average speed of 70 miles per hour. The train was hauled by King's Cross Ivatt 'Atlantic' No 3284 pulling seven Pullman cars weighing 295 tons gross. (from *The Railway Magazine*, 1934)

Summary of train services between Leeds and Britain's major cities						
Destination	Pre 1922		1969		2008	
	No of trains, one direction	Typical journey time (hr min)	No of trains, one direction	Typical journey time (hr min)	No of trains, one direction	Typical journey time (hr min)
Birmingham	7	3 25	5	2 50	16	1 59
Bristol	6	5 30	4	4 35	15	3 30
Edinburgh	3	5 02	1	4 13	14	3 10
Glasgow	4	5 12	3	5 00	2	4 20
Liverpool	8	2 13	13	2 02	15	1 49
London	13	4 00	15	3 09	32	2 23
Manchester	9	1 25 X	15	1 10 X	62	0 59 X
	7	2 05 S	17	1 26 S	39	1 30 S
Newcastle	4	2 39	7	2 00	26	1 37
Sheffield	11	1 00 X	14	1 05 X	45	0 55 X
	7	1 43 S	14	1 30 S	35	1 20 S
X = express service, S = stopping train. Only through trains are shown						

Cinema coach

The cinema coach that the LNER introduced on the Leeds-Edinburgh service on March 2 embodied a number of improvements on the pioneer London-Leeds vehicle of last year. The second coach is over 60 feet long and is divided into two sections, one for the audience and the other for the projection. There are seats for 32 persons arranged on a double row on each side with the floor of the carriage rising towards the rear. Projection is from the rear with a screen 4 feet by 5 feet. The films are non-inflammable with special materials used to reduce train noise to a minimum. (from *The Railway Magazine*, 1936)

Named trains serving Leeds		
Train	Destinations served	Approx period of operation
'The Bradford Executive (1)	Bradford-London King's Cross (KX)	1973-1984
'The Cornishman'	Bradford-Leeds-Penzance	1965-2002
'The Devonian'	Bradford-Leeds-Paignton	1927-2002
'The Dorset Scot'	Edinburgh-Leeds-Bournemouth	1999-2002
'Harrogate Sunday Pullman'	London KX-Harrogate/Bradford	1927-1960
'The Leeds Executive'	Leeds-London KX	1973-1985
'The North Briton'	Leeds-Edinburgh-Glasgow	1949-1975
'The Queen of Scots' (2)	London KX-Leeds-Edinburgh-Glasgow	1927-1964
'The Scarborough Spa Express'	Harrogate-Leeds-Scarborough (steam specials)	from 1981
'The Thames-Clyde Express'	London St Pancras-Leeds-Glasgow	1927-1975
'The Thames-Forth Express' (3)	London St Pancras-Leeds-Edinburgh	1927-1957
'The Transpennine'	Liverpool-Leeds-Hull	1961-1969
'The West Riding' (4)	Leeds/Bradford-London KX	1949-1966
'The West Yorkshire Executive'	London KX-Leeds	1984-1988
'The White Rose' (5) (6)	London KX-Leeds/Bradford	1949-1964
'The Yorkshire Pullman'	Harrogate/Bradford/Leeds -London KX	1935-2004

Notes

(1) Originally routed via Wortley Curve but later diverted via Leeds with reversal. (2) Previously 'Harrogate Pullman' 1923-1927. (3) Ran as 'The Waverley' 1957-1969. (4) Previously 'West Riding Pullman' 1925-1935, 'West Riding Limited' 1937-1939. (5) 'The White Rose Pullman' 1964-1967 (6) 'White Rose' name used for Leeds to KX trains using Eurostar units, 2002-2005

The top ex-LMS named train was 'The Thames-Clyde Express', which ran between London St Pancras and Glasgow St Enoch. Seen here in BR days in 1960, the train, behind No 46145 *The Duke of Wellington's Regiment (West Riding)*, is passing Calverley.
D. K. Jones

Above: 'The West Riding' and the 'Yorkshire Pullman' were the crack ex-LNER trains to London. Here Peppercorn Class 'A1' No 60123 *H. A. Ivatt*, in mint condition, carries 'The West Riding' nameboard at Copley Hill shed in the early 1950s. It also displays the 37B shed plate indicating it is a Copley Hill engine. The shed had an allocation of a number of these locomotives for working the crack London trains. After being oiled, watered and coaled, the locomotive would back down onto its train at Leeds Central station. *Transport Treasury*

Below: The LNER developed express rail travel with Pullman coaches and trains of ordinary corridor stock. Here a Class 'A3' 'Pacific' heads a Leeds to London King's Cross express through Ardsley in 1948, the first year of British Railways. The 'A3' was developed from Gresley's original GNR 'Pacific' design. *M. Bentley*

Above: **During the rebuilding of Leeds City station in 1961, a Class 101 DMU leaves for the west in 1961. The ugly train shed extension to the station has been removed, revealing the handsome original New station façade. Note the original Leeds station nameboard and the demolition on the left of the connecting roof between the former New and Wellington stations.** *Stations UK*

Right: **A rare visitor to Leeds: Class 50 diesel locomotive No 50040 *Leviathan* prepares to return home on an inter-city express to Plymouth in 1985. These locomotives were built in 1957 and originally leased to British Railways for hauling the Crewe to Glasgow West Coast services. Upon electrification of that route they were transferred to the Western Region.** *Author*

Right: **A Class 47 locomotive waits at the head of an inter-city train for North Wales at Leeds station in 1986. These trains were part of trans-Pennine services, but were later cut back to run only as far as Manchester.** *Author*

Regional train services

As most Leeds suburban stations were closed in the 1960s many stopping trains were withdrawn and those that continued to run made few stops within Leeds. Metro then reversed transport policy and began to develop rail transport with the result that many more trains were operated into Leeds to meet the increased demand for rail travel.

This was the result of the growth of Leeds as a regional and financial centre, with many more jobs created in the city centre. The pattern of commuting changed, with Leeds becoming dominant as the focus for regional rail services. People began to commute into Leeds over much longer distances, but despite this, and the opening of four new stations, Leeds is still poorly served by rail with currently no suburban stations at all on two of the seven lines into Leeds. According to a 1999 survey, only 2.75 million passengers used Leeds suburban stations annually. Regional services now dominate and need to continue to be developed, but also required is greater access to and from the outlying areas of the city and more new stations for the Leeds suburbs are again being considered.

Since privatisation there have been a number of changes to railway company franchises, and these are shown in the table.

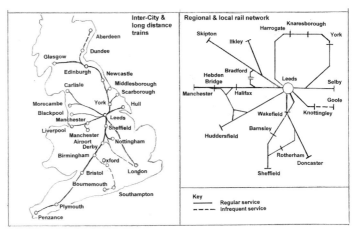

Inter-city and regional trains serving Leeds

Privatised railway franchises for routes serving Leeds			
Route	**Brand name**	**Dates operated**	**Franchise owner**
Inter-city East Coast	Great North Eastern Railway	1996-2007	Sea Containers
	National Express East Coast	2007-2009	National Express
Inter-city Cross Country	Virgin Cross Country	1997-2007	Virgin
	Cross Country	2007 onwards	Arriva
Midland main line	Midland Main Line	1996-2007	National Express
	East Midland Trains	2007 onwards	Stagecoach
Regional Railways North East	Northern Spirit*	1997-2000	MTL Rail
	Arriva Northern	2000-2004	Arriva
	Northern Rail	2004 onwards	Serco/NedRailways
Trans-Pennine**	Trans-Pennine Express	2003 onwards	First/Keolis
* Northern Spirit brand name introduced 1998			
** Trans-Pennine franchise created 2003 by removing trans-Pennine trains from Arriva Northern franchise			

Excursion and holiday trains

From the outset the railways catered for excursion traffic that could not be met by regular services. These were mainly to holiday and tourist destinations for day trips and longer stays. In the early days most people did not travel much except for occasional day trips, particularly at Bank Holidays, or annual holidays when the mills and factories shut down for two weeks in August. The railways kept spare rolling stock especially for this traffic; it was usually antiquated coaching stock, much of which was parked in sidings at local stations when not required.

Holiday travel was therefore very big business for the railways, and always, unlike today, took place on Saturdays. A service the railways offered was 'Luggage in Advance', whereby passengers could send their luggage a few days in advance and on return it would be delivered just after the end of the holiday.

When passenger stations closed to regular services the platform facilities were often retained for excursion traffic. Stations such as Rothwell and Robin Hood were used for specials for more than 50 years after they officially closed.

The 'Beeching Report' proposed discarding this special traffic by means of a major reduction in the provision of spare rolling stock. Despite this, British Rail continued to run these trains, albeit on a reduced scale. This was achieved by using stock from Monday to Friday peak trains at weekends and on Bank Holidays. In addition BR ran inter-city long-distance day trips under the 'Merrymaker' banner to major tourist resorts such as Margate, Dunoon and the Isle of Wight.

However, with rail privatisation this has now come to an end, with only a very few excursions now being operated by specialist train operators.

A handbill for a 1949 excursion to Belle Vue, Manchester. This was unusual as most excursions started at Leeds, but this originated at Guiseley and reversed at Leeds before continuing to pick up passengers.

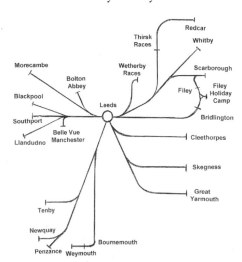

Popular destinations for excursion and summer Saturday holiday trains from Leeds

Emigrant specials

An interesting phase of the traffic dealt with at Leeds New station is the frequent running of emigrant specials from Hull, NER, to Liverpool, LNWR, by way of Leeds. The heavy train loads of Continental emigrants 'en route' to America formed a picture not likely to be soon erased from the mind. (from *The Railway Magazine*, 1915)

Top: **People used the railways in large numbers at holiday times. Here a group of holidaymakers poses for the cameraman of the local newspaper at Morley Top station while waiting for a Morley Feast Week holiday special to Cleethorpes in August 1958.** *Stephen White/Leslie Overend*

Above: **1970s railway excursion leaflets**

Right: **Steam was phased out by British Railways in 1968 but it was not long before main-line steam specials were being run. These were very popular and large crowds turned out to see them. Frequent destinations were Carlisle and Scarborough, and here ex-LNER 2-6-2 Class 'V2' No 4771 Green Arrow departs from Leeds for the north in 1977.** *Author*

Night trains and sleeper services

The railway was and still is a 24-hour operator. Local services and branches generally operate from 06.00 to 24.00, but on the main lines night trains continue to operate, although to a changed pattern. When journey times were longer much travel was at night, with trains operating on most routes.

Sleeper services ran until the 1980s to London and Glasgow. The London service was particularly popular with MPs, and I remember seeing Denis Healey boarding the sleeper at Leeds. As trains became faster the demand for night travel diminished.

Additionally, Royal Mail and newspapers were transported during the night on both special mail and scheduled passenger trains. Night trains still operate on the York to Manchester Airport route through Leeds, as do some freight trains.

Above: **A BR Eastern Region promotion for the autumn of 1975**

Right: **A 'Happily Family' ticket from Morley to Filey and return, July 1975**

Timetables, tickets and promotions

The railways invented the timetable to show people when trains were running, and have always promoted rail travel through posters, leaflets and special offers. In particular, the railway companies promoted holiday resorts through many famous posters.

The basic cost of rail travel has often been quite high, but the railway companies promoted travel to maximise their revenue. For the commuter special early morning workmen's fares were available until about the 1960s, and season tickets in many forms have always been available.

Off-peak travel has more recently been promoted and made cheaper in an effort to fill empty seats in the middle of the day. Some examples of tickets and promotions are shown here.

A major campaign to secure the long-term future of local trains was launched by the Eastern Region of British Railways. This involved marketing the trains as a 'West Riding' network of 15 routes, 452 route miles and 78 stations. Each route was given a name and colour code, together with travel incentives such as 'Bullseye' season tickets centred on Leeds, and 'Happy Family' tickets to Harrogate, York and East Coast resorts for off-peak day trips.

Local rail travel was boosted by the introduction of diesel multiple units in the late 1950s, but this was curtailed by Beeching's axe. The 'West Riding' campaign was therefore very significant as it reversed the policy of the 1960s by promoting rather than running down local train services. The campaign was an immediate success, becoming the start of the long haul back for local trains, which continued with the formation of Passenger Transport Executives for West and South Yorkshire.

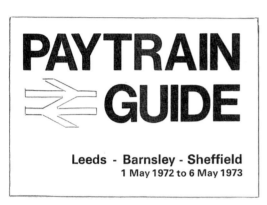

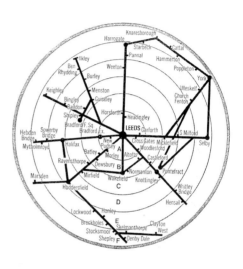

Above: Lines with unmanned stations were promoted as 'Paytrain' routes.

Above: Bullseye season ticket zones

Left: WYPTE heavily promoted off-peak travel as a means of filling empty seats in the middle of the day. This is an 'Off Peak It' promotion from 1982.

Right: WYPTE promotions: the 'Saver Strip' was a bus multi-journey ticket cancelled by a machine fitted at every MetroTrain station. The 'Metro Card' was and still is a season ticket allowing bus and rail travel. Initially this was linked to the 'Bullseye' ticket with zones outside West Yorkshire, but later the number of zones was reduced.

Below: A Class 144 unit forms a Leeds to Huddersfield local service calling at Cottingley station in 1988, shortly after opening. On the right a passenger can be seen operating the 'Kerching' ticket-cancelling machine, which were installed on

Metro has just the ticket for you

DayRover
For a great day out

With a DayRover you can make as many journeys as you like in any one day . . . any day you choose.

DayRovers are valid on all buses and MetroTrains in West Yorkshire. There are four to choose from. Pick the one that's right for you.

From Metro Travel Centres, Bus Station Sales Outlets, staffed British Rail Stations, Post Offices, selected Newsagents and selected Travel Agents.

SaverStrip
For 2 free rides

Twelve rides for the price of 10. Buy it from one of the 1,300 outlets in West Yorkshire and 'Kerching' it on any bus or MetroTrain in West Yorkshire.

Select the SaverStrip for the value of fare you normally pay e.g. if your journey usually costs you 30p ask for a £3 SaverStrip.

On sale from Metro Travel Centres, Bus Station Sales Outlets, staffed British Rail Stations, Post Offices and selected Newsagents.

MetroCard
For regular bus/rail users

The value-for-money ticket for those who travel every day. It's valid on buses and MetroTrains for a week, a month, 3 months or a year.

And each one offers exceptional savings on the normal fare. In fact, the more you travel, the more you save! There's also a special MetroCard for students.

Available from Metro Travel Centres, Bus Station Sales Outlets, staffed British Rail Stations and Post Offices.

every West Yorkshire station. The tickets got their nickname from the noise of the machine as it clipped a notch out of the bus-type 'Saver Strip' ticket. Unfortunately the machines suffered from vandalism and the system was replaced by ordinary season tickets. *Author*

Football and sports specials

Being a mass transit carrier the railways have always catered for people travelling to big sporting occasions. For many years special trains were run, but in the 1970s problems began to be encountered with unruly behaviour by supporters. This led to vandalism, with some trains being damaged, requiring police escorts to be provided. In 1980 an FA Cup semi-final between Everton and West Ham was played at Elland Road. Ten special trains were run and the police used an unusual tactic to keep the two clubs' fans apart. The trains from London were run into Leeds City station and the trains from Liverpool into Morley station, then both sets of fans had a police-escorted walk of 2 miles to the ground.

In the 1950s the closed stations of Beeston and Farnley & Wortley were retained for many years to cater for football fans when trains made special stops. There was a proposal to open a new station at Elland Road in 1986, but this never materialised. Today people have to use Leeds or Cottingley stations for football at Elland Road, but for cricket test matches at Headingley Northern Rail still operates a quarter-hourly augmented service between Leeds and Horsforth for cricket fans to alight at either Headingley or Burley Park.

The Railway Clearing House

This was set up in 1842 to apportion revenue between the various railway companies for both passenger and freight traffics. It was in response to a growing national network where through journeys were made by passengers using a number of different train companies' services, and private freight wagons travelled on other companies' lines. With the Grouping in 1923 the work of the RCH was greatly reduced, and with nationalisation in 1948 it was no longer required.

Tickets were always collected at the end of each journey at the ticket barriers of the main Leeds stations. At the suburban Leeds stations the porter would meet every train, with his lamp after dark, to inspect and collect tickets from alighting passengers. These would then all be sent to the RCH office in London for the receipts from the tickets to be divided between the various railway companies. Passengers were never allowed to keep their used tickets. It was only in later British Railways days that passengers were allowed to keep tickets, as open and unmanned stations became prevalent and compensation could be claimed for severely late trains.

In today's privatised railway a similar process for dividing revenue between train companies is used, but this is now done quite easily by commuter.

A Class 141 unit forming a Harrogate to Leeds service calls at Headingly station in 1987. Passengers can alight here for the famous football and cricket grounds. On test match days a special Leeds to Horsforth augmented service is operated. *Author*

7
Locomotives and rolling stock

Locomotives and units

Initially the railways used small locomotives hauling modestly sized trucks and carriages, but as traffic developed locomotives became larger and trains heavier and longer. The LNER used 'Pacific' (4-6-2) locomotives for its crack trains, with 0-6-2 and 4-4-2 tank engines for the local trains, while the LMS stuck with 4-6-0 types for the expresses, but had more modern 2-6-2 or 2-6-4 tank locomotives for the locals.

In the 1930s, to reduce costs, experiments were made with steam railcars; they were tried on many lightly used services, particularly on the Gildersome branch and between Leeds Central and Castleford. Push-pull trains were also used.

Train crews in steam days required two men per locomotive plus a guard. The second man had to gain many years' experience as a fireman before qualifying as a driver. Because of the long journey times and to avoid working excessive hours, some train crews did 'lodging' turns, which involved a stay-over at the destination. The LMS provided hostels at Farnley Junction (42 beds) and Holbeck (20 beds) for incoming drivers and firemen. With the arrival of diesel and electric traction, locomotives eventually became single-manned.

Both railway and tramway staff from Leeds served in the two World Wars, with many killed or injured. The tramways employed female conductors for the first time during the First World War, while on the railways it was the late 1990s before women became regularly employed as both train drivers and conductors.

Initially both railwaymen and tram crews were poorly paid and worked long hours. Trade unions were formed with the result that occasional strikes were held to improve working conditions. Most notable were the 1926 General Strike, a tramway strike during the Second World War, and the damaging ASLEF train drivers' strike of 1955, which was taken advantage of by road transport interests.

In 1954 a trial pilot scheme of diesel multiple units (DMUs) was introduced from Leeds Central to Bradford, Harrogate and Castleford. This was hugely successful, resulting in the 1955 Modernisation Plan, which envisaged the complete replacement of steam by diesel with all local services going over to DMUs and diesel locomotives used on long-distance passenger and freight trains. 'Deltic' locomotives were the mainstay of the London service until the arrival of the High Speed Train in 1978.

Early steam sheds were provided near Holbeck station and at Central and Wellington stations, but as the railways expanded they were moved further out from the centre to

GNR locomotive development, 1848-1922: these locomotives were employed on the Leeds to London express trains. As trains became heavier and faster the power requirement increased, resulting in larger locomotives being built until the ultimate 'Pacific' type, which operated until the end of steam.

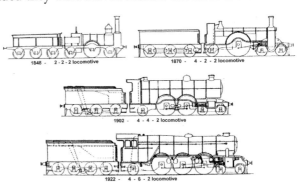

1848 - 2 - 2 - 2 locomotive

1870 - 4 - 2 - 2 locomotive

1902 - 4 - 4 - 2 locomotive

1922 - 4 - 6 - 2 locomotive

larger depots. Originally the LYR had a small locomotive shed at Copley Hill but later served Leeds from the motive power depot at Low Moor in Bradford.

Most popular locomotives and units used on Leeds passenger rail services	
Railway company	**Types of motive power**
NER	Classes 'G5' 0-4-4T, 'D20' 4-4-0, 'B16' 4-6-0
GNR	Classes 'C1' 4-4-2, 'C12' 4-4-2T, 'G2' 0-4-4T, 'N1' 0-6-2T
MR	Classes '2P' and '4P' 4-4-0
LNWR	Classes '4' and '5XP' 4-6-0
LYR	Classes '2P' 2-4-2T
LNER	Classes 'A3' 4-6-2, 'B1' 4-6-0, 'C13' 4-4-2T (ex-GCR), 'D49' 4-4-0, 'V2' 2-6-2
LMS	Class '2' and '3' 2-6-2T, '4' 2-6-4T, '5' 4-6-0, '5XP' and '6', 'Patriot', 'Jubilee' and 'Royal Scot' 4-6-0
BR	Steam: Classes 'A1' 4-6-2, Standard '5' 4-6-0
	DMUs: Classes 101, 102, 104, 108, 111, 114, 124 (Trans-Pennine), 141, 142, 144, 150, 153, 155, 156, 158
	Diesel locos: Classes 40, 43 (HST), 44, 45, 46, 47, 55 ('Deltic')
	EMUs: Class 321
	Electric loco: Class 91
Northern Rail	Class 333 EMUs
Cross Country	Classes 220, 221 DMUs
Trans-Pennine	Classes 170, 185 DMUs
Note: LNER and LMS class designations are used for pre-Grouping locos.	

Liveries of passenger trains					
Railway company	Locomotives	Coaches	Railway company	Locomotives	Coaches
GCR	Brunswick green/black	Teak	NER	Saxony green/black	Teak
GNR	Apple green/black	Teak	LNER	Apple green/black	Teak
LNWR	Black	White and carmine lake	LMS	Crimson lake/black	Red
LYR	Black	Brown and lake	BR	Brunswick green	Carmine and cream
MR	Crimson lake	Crimson lake		Medium blue/black	Maroon
				Blue*	Blue and grey*
Company	Livery	Company	Livery		
GNER	Blue and red	East Coast	White and grey		
MML	Teal, green and tangerine	Northern	Blue and purple		
Northern Spirit/Arriva	Aqua blue	Cross Country	Maroon and silver		
Virgin	Red and silver	East Midland	Red, orange and blue		
Trans-Pennine	Blue				
* As BR moved towards privatisation rolling stock was later painted in short-lived Sector liveries.					

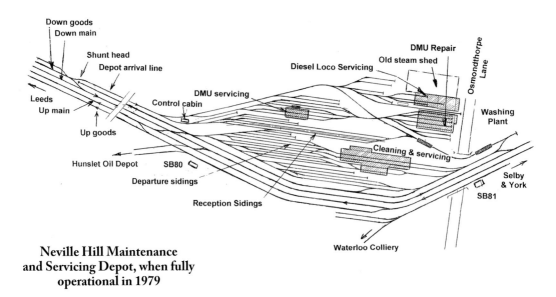

Neville Hill Maintenance and Servicing Depot, when fully operational in 1979

Below: The LNER era: the top link passenger locomotives of the LNER were four classes of 'Pacific' locomotives developed from Nigel Gresley's original 4-6-2 type for the GNR. However, Gresley's most successful locomotive was the streamlined Class 'A4', and here No 4495 *Golden Fleece* leaves Leeds Central with a train for King's Cross. *Transport Treasury*

The Leeds locomotive depots were:

Companies	Location	Closed	Companies	Location	Closed
GNR/LNER	Ardsley	1965	MR/LMS	Holbeck	1986
GNR/LNER	Copley Hill	1964	NER/LNER	Neville Hill	-
LNWR/LMS	Farnley Junction	1966	MR/LMS	Stourton	1967

With the end of steam most of these depots were closed as diesels were much easier to service, and many train services were being withdrawn. All DMUs, coaching stock and some locomotives were maintained and serviced at an enlarged Neville Hill depot. Holbeck remained open for locomotives but was closed in the 1980s as more trains became DMUs.

However, with expanded rail services Northern Rail reopened the depot in 2006 for the additional servicing of DMUs.

Electrification came late to the Leeds area, but the Doncaster and Ilkley lines are now operated by modern electric multiple units (EMUs), with London trains hauled by Class 91 electric locomotives.

Left: **The last-built LNER locomotive, Class 'A2' No 525 *A. H. Peppercorn*, leaves Leeds Central in 1948 shortly after nationalisation. The 'A2s' originated from a rebuild by Edward Thompson of Gresley's 2-8-2 type, later developed further by Peppercorn.** *Transport Treasury*

Right: **The Class 'D49' 4-4-0 locomotives were designed in 1927 by Gresley for lighter express duties, and were employed on Newcastle to Liverpool services. However, after the war they were used extensively on local services around Leeds. Here a locomotive of the class takes the spur to Leeds Central at Gelderd Junction in BR days with the Harrogate portion of the 'Yorkshire Pullman'. The train will reverse at Central station.** *E. R. Morten collection*

Above: **LMS locomotives: unlike the LNER, the top LMS express trains into Leeds were hauled by 4-6-0 locomotives, of which the Stanier 6P 'Royal Scot' Class engines were the most powerful. Here in BR days No 46109 *Royal Engineer* waits to leave Leeds City station with the 10.35am train for Glasgow on August Bank Holiday 1959, which was the Leeds holiday week.** *Michael Mensing*

Below: **Next came the 'Jubilee' Class 5XP locomotives, and No 45568 *Western Australia* is heading a northbound express out of Leeds. Monkbridge Works is on the left and Whitehall Junction signal box on the right. The access path from Whitehall Road to the former Holbeck station can be seen in the foreground.** *D. K. Jones*

Right: **Before the arrival of the Stanier 4-6-0s, Class 4P three-cylinder compound 4-4-0 locomotives were used on ex-Midland Railway express services into Leeds. Here No 41081 is pictured passing Holbeck Low Level station in 1951 bound for Leeds with a local train.** *E. R. Morten collection*

Below right: **Arrival of British Railways: the first sign of nationalisation was when 'BRITISH RAILWAYS' started to appear on locomotives in place of 'LMS' or 'LNER'. This was later replaced by the 'Lion & Wheel' symbol. Ex-LMS Caprotti Class 5 4-6-0 No 44754 is leaving Leeds with an express just after nationalisation.** *Transport Treasury*

Below: **British Railways then embarked upon building a range of standard steam locomotives. There were 11 standard types (excluding the solitary Class 8P) and most appeared around Leeds, although not in great numbers. The BR Standard classes were based upon LMS designs and the Class 5 was the most numerous seen in Leeds. No 73158, in grimy condition near the end of the steam era, enters Leeds City station with empty coaching stock for a special train in 1965. The high running plate, which was a distinguishing feature over its LMS cousins, is seen to good effect.** *D. K. Jones*

Above: Some Standard tanks were allocated to Neville Hill. Here Class 4MT 2-6-4T No 80118 calls at Cross Gates in 1960 with an unusually long local train. It is likely that this train is for Wetherby, where the Town station was used for race traffic following the closure of the Racecourse station a year earlier. *D. K. Jones*

Below: Development of the railcar: a steam railcar is seen at Ardsley in the 1930s. These were developed between 1900 and 1930 to reduce costs on branch lines. They had a small vertical boiler in the leading coach but could be driven from either end. They were used by the LNER on services from Leeds Central to Castleford, on the Gildersome branch and on some ex-NER lines. *Morley History Society*

Right: A later development was the push-pull train. This consisted of a tank locomotive permanently attached to coaches and fitted so that it could be driven from either end without the need for turning. Ivatt Class 'C12' No 67386 was push-pull-fitted in 1949 for working the Lofthouse to Drighlington service, and is seen here after arrival at Drighlington & Adwalton station. *Morley History Society*

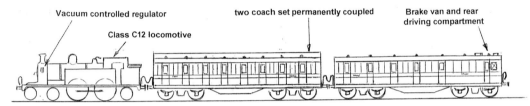

A sketch of the Gildersome branch train in 1949

Below: In 1954 British Railways introduced experimental lightweight two-car diesel multiple units to operate local services from Leeds Central to Harrogate, Bradford Exchange and Castleford. These were very successful and greatly increased patronage as well as reducing operating costs. Here one of the new units is seen at Ardsley with a Castleford service. The experiment was followed by the 1955 Modernisation Plan to replace all surviving steam services by DMUs. *Morley History Society*

Left: **Following the success of the 1954 scheme a construction programme of new DMUs was commenced to replace all local services. The most numerous type was the Metro-Cammell Class 101, and shown here is an example of the class at Leeds station in 1984 sporting the MetroTrain logo of the West Yorkshire PTE.** *Author*

Below: **By the 1980s the post-1955 build of DMUs were becoming worn out and a new replacement second-generation batch was constructed. Most of these were updated conventional DMUs of Classes 150, 155, 156 and 158. However, British Rail developed a lightweight range of units reverting to vehicles with four wheels and based upon Leyland bus technology. The first of these was the Class 141 built specially for West Yorkshire, followed by improved Classes 142 and 144. The picture shows a Class 141 unit in original green and cream livery leaving Leeds station with a service for Goole while a Class 144, in the later crimson and cream livery, is in the bay platform.** *Author*

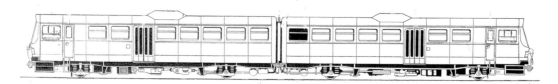

The Class 141 lightweight diesel multiple unit

Above: The next development of locomotives after the Class 55 was the building of a High Speed Train prototype. This was tested on the East Coast Main Line between Leeds and Newcastle in 1973, and is photographed here at Neville Hill depot during that year. Skelton Grange Power Station can be seen in the background. *Author*

Below: After the success of the prototype HST, many production units were built for the London and cross-country services. These went on to give outstanding service and many consider them to be BR's most successful train; they continue to operate many inter-city trains today. A GNER-operated HST passes Ardsley with a London express in 1995. *Author*

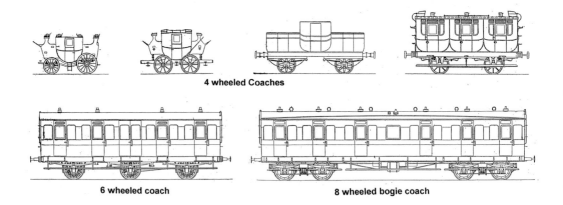

4 wheeled Coaches

6 wheeled coach   8 wheeled bogie coach

Above: The development of passenger coaches, in this case LYR. The first coaches had compartments only, then a corridor between the compartments was provided within each coach. Toilets were the next addition, and the next development was a connection between coaches so that passengers could walk the length of the train. Coaches then went on to have kitchens and dining facilities, sleeping berths and even became Travelling Post Offices.

Railway carriages

Passenger railway carriages developed from the first four-wheel types to larger six-wheelers and eventually to today's modern bogie coaches. Initially they were constructed with wooden bodies on steel frames, but the designs were gradually developed to improve safety. In 1949 British Railways standardised on an all-steel coach. Trains progressively became heavier, offering better facilities for the passenger and improved comfort. The first sleeping car was introduced on the East Coast route in 1873 and the first kitchen car by the GNR in 1879.

As with engine sheds, carriage depots and servicing facilities were initially at the city centre stations, but were later concentrated at Wortley (LNWR/LMS), Copley Hill (GNR/LNER) and Neville Hill (NER/LNER). Most MR carriage servicing was done at Bradford Market Street (later Forster Square).

Lighting of carriages was initially by compressed gas, carried in cylinders mounted under the carriage frames. Unfortunately this proved to be dangerous in the case of a train crash resulting in the burning of the wooden carriages. With the advent of electricity it became attractive to provide lighting by this means. Early attempts were not too successful due to difficulties with generators in guard's vans and dynamos affected by train speed. It was the introduction of the 'Stone system' at the turn of the 20th century that led to all trains being fitted with this standard electric lighting.

Locomotive lamps and headcodes

In steam days locomotives carried headlamp codes in order that signalmen could identify trains and give the necessary priority. There were ten categories of train from A to H, J and K and each had a distinct headcode. These were composed of white-painted oil lamps, and when diesels arrived the practice was continued but with white disks. Later still a new four-digit identification number was introduced, and new diesel locomotives and DMUs were fitted with number panels. However, as the railways began to be controlled by a few power signal boxes the system was abandoned and the panels were plated over. Signalmen controlling trains today still use similar reporting numbers, but they are not seen by the public.

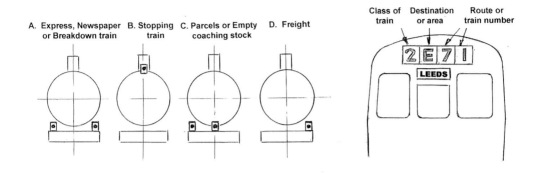

Locomotive headcodes
There were ten different headcodes for trains of Classes A to H, J and K – these were the most popular. A number panel on a DMU is also shown.

Trains also had to carry a red tail-light for safety reasons, and unless it was working and visible the train could not run. Again, this was an oil lamp, and was even used on DMUs, even though they had their own electric lights. Trains continued to carry a separate independent tail-light until the end of the 20th century, when they were allowed to use their own tail-lights, although these now have two lights instead of a single one.

Personal reminiscences

After the end of the Second World War there was a period of austerity and a popular cheap hobby was 'trainspotting'. Being at school during this period I joined most other boys in this hobby, although in my case it went much deeper than simply collecting locomotive numbers and involved a keen interest in the engineering side of railways.

I spent many hours at Gildersome watching the trains go by, both at the ex-GNR station and, following a walk over the fields to the western tunnel portal, on the Leeds New line. I therefore had a choice of LNER or LMS, and can remember the railways being nationalised, but could see no reason for it.

A popular day out was to catch a bus to Leeds and alight at Farnley for a shed tour. First on the list was Farnley Junction, where no one ever raised any objection to us going all round the shed taking every engine number. Then followed a walk to Copley Hill, where trains could be seen from the adjacent Wortley Park. There was a very strict regime here, the only access to the shed being via a long flight of steps beyond which we were never able to passed. I was at Copley Hill one memorable early evening when three brand-new Class 'A1' locomotives arrived from Doncaster. They made a very impressive sight, coupled together in LNER Apple green livery with 'BRITISH RAILWAYS' on their tenders but, I believe, unnamed at that time.

After Copley Hill it was a short walk to Holbeck depot, although we always called it 'Nineveh' in those days. Again you could walk round the shed collecting numbers without much trouble. A further short walk brought us to a popular vantage point at the side of the track at the triangle just outside Leeds City station. Spotters used to sit in a concrete ballast bunker and you could almost touch the trains, which would never be allowed today. After a few hours of watching the trains it was home after a good day out.

8
Freight depots and sidings

In the early years of the railways almost everything was transported by rail. Motor transport began to develop at the beginning of the 20th century, but the monopoly of the railway in transporting goods was largely maintained until after the end of the Second World War. From the 1950s road transport competition began to bite, encouraged by Government policy and resulting in Beeching abandoning large amounts of freight traffic, while the decline of the coal industry reduced originating coal traffic. Newspaper, parcel and mail business survived on rail until the 1990s, but today very little freight traffic remains in the Leeds area.

The map opposite shows the extent of the freight facilities that existed within the Leeds boundary, which can be categorised as follows:

Local stations: The vast majority of local railway stations provided both passenger and freight facilities. Exceptions included Churwell (on an embankment) and Osmondthorpe (built to serve a housing estate).

Leeds city centre depots and warehouses: There were extensive railway facilities close to the central Leeds area catering for goods dispatched to and from the city centre.

Perishable traffic: The railways carried extensive perishable traffic such as vegetables, milk and fish.

Livestock: This was dispatched to the Cattle Market at Holbeck. Racehorses were transported to Wetherby Racecourse in special horsebox vans sometimes attached to passenger trains. Racing pigeons were carried from local stations by normal passenger trains to an organised release station.

Colliery sidings: Almost all the numerous pits in the area were connected to the rail network for outward transport of coal.

Foundry and engineering works: All these had a siding for the inward supply of raw materials and outward flow of finished products.

Power stations: These received coal or oil shipments. Kirkstall and Skelton Grange were built as coal-fired stations but Kirkstall was converted to oil in the 1960s.

Royal Mail and newspaper traffic: Mail was sorted in Travelling Post Office trains, which ran overnight, as did newspaper trains. Smaller consignments of both were also conveyed in the guards' vans of ordinary passenger trains.

Parcels traffic: The railways carried large amounts of parcels both for Royal Mail and the railway's own parcel service. Later this was branded as Red Star Parcels.

Theatrical traffic: The railway companies had special departments that conveyed passengers, scenery, theatrical companies and circuses. These often took the form of special trains, which usually operated on a Sunday.

Oil traffic: Oil trains ran to Kirkstall Power Station until closure in 1968. The Hunslet East oil terminal was opened in 1967 and received block oil trains from refineries on the Mersey and Humber until closure in 2001.

Stone traffic: The railways carried the output from a number of quarries, particularly those at Woodkirk and Robin Hood. From 1977 to about 2005 Marsh Lane was used as a depot for incoming constructional stone traffic. Later this was transferred to terminals at Leeds Stourton and Hunslet East after the closure of the oil terminal.

Containers and block trains: The only major rail freight flows to have survived are block train workings of Freightliner containers from Stourton, stone aggregate trains from quarries in the Yorkshire Dales and Peak District, and coal trains from Scotland via the old Midland route passing through Leeds to the Aire Valley power stations.

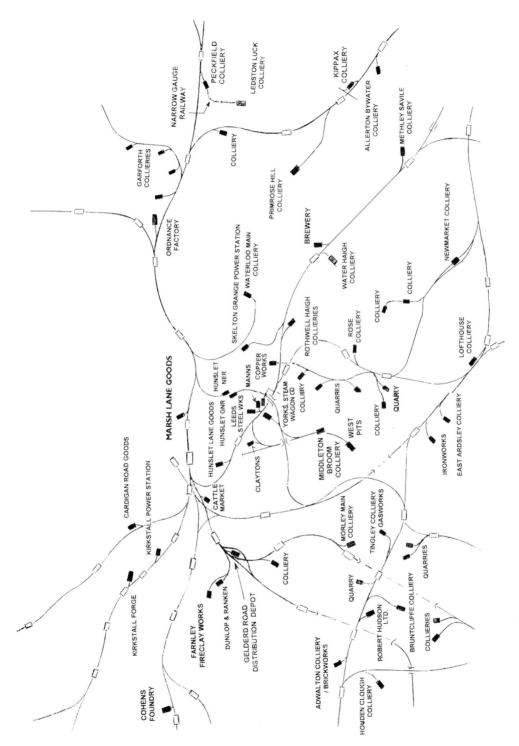

Colliery and works railway sidings in Leeds industrial areas

Two examples of wagon labels that were attached to railway wagons to show their destination. One shows incoming potatoes to Leeds Wellington, and the other was used for dispatching goods from the Middleton Railway's siding at Hunslet.

Delivery and collection at local stations was by road, as shown on this GNR poster.

Wagonload freight

Until Beeching most rail freight was in wagonload trains. Freight was loaded into wagons at local railway stations then taken by the 'pick-up' freight train to a marshalling yard where the wagons were sorted into new trains for their destination.

Some factories dispatched whole trains of their products. One such, shown here, is a 200-ton load of Robert Hudson railway equipment leaving Gildersome station. It is likely that this is during the First World War as Hudson's dispatched vast amounts of railway materials for the war effort. Most of Hudson's output was normally sent as wagonload traffic via the pick-up freight train.

Coal traffic

Local railways served the numerous collieries in Leeds and carried vast amounts of coal. In the early industrial era there were many rail-served small collieries, but these were progressively closed as coal seams were exhausted and production became concentrated on the larger mechanised pits. Early closures were Kippax in 1904 and Morley Main in 1909, with the Garforth collieries ceasing production in the 1930s. Eleven Leeds collieries were taken over

A GNR train of 200 tons of Hudson track at Gildersome station after loading at the Gildersome Foundry. The picture appeared in a Robert Hudson catalogue.

by the National Coal Board in 1948. All were served by main-line railways except at Ledston Luck, where coal was conveyed in mine cars by a 2ft 6in narrow-gauge surface railway to Peckfield Colliery for washing and dispatch. The last Leeds mine to close was at Allerton Bywater in 1992. Originating coal traffic therefore ceased in 1992, although coal trains continued to pass through Leeds; today the only examples are those carrying imported coal from the docks to the Aire Valley power stations.

Zoo special train

The LNER recently conveyed a complete zoo by special train from Leeds to Glasgow. The special consisted of 17 vans of wild animals (including camels, elephants, zebras, snakes, monkeys etc), five caravans, stores and a motor tractor, the total weight being 515 tons. Many of the cages and caravans were so bulky that the special had to be run at a restricted speed and stops made at intervals for examination. (from *The Railway Magazine*, 1929)

Red Star Parcels

The railways carried large amounts of parcel traffic. However, in 1986 British Rail lost the contract for Royal Mail parcels, but continued with its own parcel service under the Red Star banner. This was privatised in 1995 but did not survive long before the business was surrendered to road transport.

A 1977 advert for British Rail's Red Star 'station to station' express parcel business.

Above: **An 0-6-0 saddle tank heads an East & West Yorkshire Union Railway goods train near Robin Hood in 1923. The locomotive was one of a number built for the company by Manning Wardle in Leeds; they became Classes 'J84' and 'J85' when taken over by the LNER. The train is typical of the period, composed of four-wheeled short-wheelbase wagons.** *LCGB, Ken Nunn collection*

Pigeon special trains

The LNER carried over 400,000 pigeons during the past season in special pigeon expresses. (from *The Railway Magazine*, 1925)

'Speedlink'

Beeching proposed the ending of wagonload traffic, but in an effort to retain the business British Rail set up a streamlined 'Speedlink' service. This consisted of wagonload traffic using a network of 12 main yards, 17 section sidings and 23 terminals. This worked well for a number of years but the network was abandoned in 1991 for financial reasons.

Leeds freight facility closures

The accompanying table gives the approximate years of closure of the main freight facilities that served the Leeds area. Precise dates are quite complicated as sometimes lines were mothballed or remained open for dismantling so that often the official

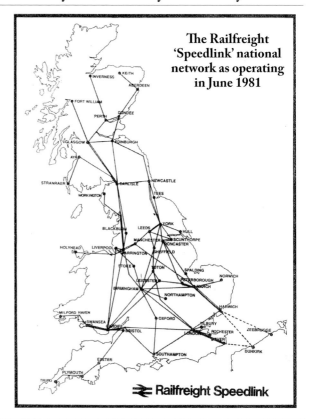

The Railfreight 'Speedlink' national network as operating in June 1981

≹ **Railfreight Speedlink**

Year of closure	Stations closed	Year of closure	Stations closed
1959	Morley Low (Goods)	1975	Gelderd Road Distribution Depot (Cadbury)
1960	Tingley (G), Farnley & Wortley (G)	1981	Peckfield Colliery
1962	Beeston (G)	1983	Armley Moor (G), Rothwell Colliery
1963	Armley Canal Rd (G), Newlay & Horsforth (G), Gildersome (LNWR)	1984	Hunslet Balm Road siding, Methley Saville Colliery
1964	Tingley-Woodkirk line; Yeadon branch, Arthington (G)	1986	Ledston Luck Colliery, Royal Mail Parcels
1966	Lofthouse N Junction-Stourton line; Hunslet NER goods depot; Gildersome branch, Wetherby (G)	1990	Whitehall Road Goods
1967	Beeston Junction-Hunslet (GNR) line	1991	Dunlop & Ranken (Farnley branch)
1968	Calverley & Rodley (G), Farnley & Wortley (G), Guiseley (G), East Ardsley Colliery, Waterloo Main Colliery, Middleton Broom Colliery	1992	Allerton Bywater Colliery
1969	Tingley-Morley Top (G), Bramley (G), Ardsley (G)	1996	Hunslet Engine Co siding
1970	Kirkstall Coal Depot, Tingley Gas Works, Primrose Hill Colliery, Water Haigh Colliery	1997	Red Star Parcels, Royal Mail letters and newspapers
1972	Hunslet Lane Depot; Cardigan Road Depot	2001	Hunslet East Oil terminal
1974	Wellington Street Goods (NER/GNR)	2005	Marsh Lane stone siding

closure date is well after traffic ceased. Also some depots and sidings reopened, such as Whitehall Road and Hunslet Balm Road. Of the small stations, freight traffic sometimes ceased at the same time as the station closed to passengers, but at others goods traffic continued. However, it is hoped that this gives a general indication of the run-down of local freight facilities.

Personal reminiscences of railway freight

Just after the Second World War most freight was carried by the railways, with the roads being relatively quiet. I experienced at first hand the extensive freight operation and the efficient way that goods were transported by rail.

There was heavy trans-Pennine freight movement comprising many goods trains that came from the NER area through Leeds City station to the ex-LNWR yard at Copley Hill, then taking either the route through Morley or at busy times the Leeds New line. Both these lines were heavily graded and these trains usually had an ex-LMS 0-8-0 freight locomotive at the front, with another locomotive at the back to assist it up the bank. When I lived at Morley I often watched these freight trains during the day, but at night you could still hear them.

I particularly remember that there was a night train at about 11.30pm that used the Leeds New line. I would lay in bed and hear the locomotives struggling up the gradient from Farnley Junction until the train plunged into the tunnel at Gildersome. There would then be a quiet period until the train exited the tunnel and you could hear it further as it attacked the summit towards Birstal.

Before then I lived next to Gildersome station and observed the very heavy freight traffic on the ex-GNR branch. There was a continuous procession of coal trains from the South Yorkshire pits to feed the industrial areas of Bradford and Halifax. Gildersome station itself generated large amounts of traffic, mainly from the Robert Hudson siding. The steel train would arrive in the morning from Ardsley to deliver steel plates and sections. In the evening the pick-up freight from Bradford would attach loaded wagons, which often made up a full train load. This would then progress to Ardsley for the wagons to be sorted for their destinations, mostly for the docks and export.

Hudson's used to dispatch their standard gauge 300cu ft side-tipping wagons in normal freight trains. To do this they had to get special permission for a 'one-off' trip and the bodies had to be specially locked in position. Hundreds of these wagons were supplied and could be seen at every colliery where they were used for transporting the colliery waste from pit head to slag heap.

It is difficult to imagine now, but almost every station platform had trolleys full of parcels, newspapers, mail and even poultry, all transported by train. In those days the local railway was predominantly a freight carrier, while today it is heavily passenger-orientated.

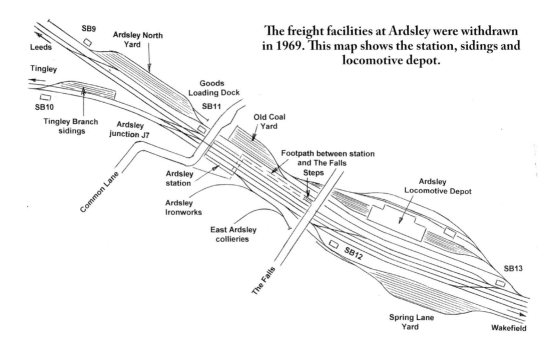

The freight facilities at Ardsley were withdrawn in 1969. This map shows the station, sidings and locomotive depot.

SB9
Ardsley North Yard
Leeds
Tingley
Goods Loading Dock
SB10
SB11
Tingley Branch sidings
Ardsley junction J7
Old Coal Yard
Common Lane
Ardsley station
Footpath between station and The Falls Steps
Ardsley Locomotive Depot
Ardsley Ironworks
East Ardsley collieries
The Falls
SB12
SB13
Spring Lane Yard
Wakefield

Below: A Leeds to Sheffield train formed of a Class 144 DMU passes the Ardsley station site in 1997. The extensive layout shown above has all gone, with the trackwork reduced to two tracks only. Large numbers of new houses have now been built on the old sidings and motive power depot, making a reopened station a logical development. It can be seen that the old station bridge has been raised to accommodate the overhead wires. *Author*

Railways in east and south-east Leeds, showing many of the lost goods facilities.

For the names of the junctions, signal boxes and level crossings coded 'J', 'SB' and 'LC', see pages 97 and 98.

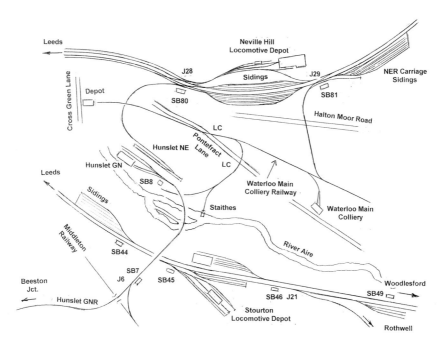

Ex-LMS 8F 2-8-0 No 48083 has a backdrop Holbeck motive power depot as it passes Engine Shed Junction signal box around 1960 and crosses from the Whitehall curve to the slow lines with a southbound freight of empty wagons. There were very heavy freight movements on the Midland main line between the Shipley and Hunslet lines avoiding Leeds City station. *David Hey*

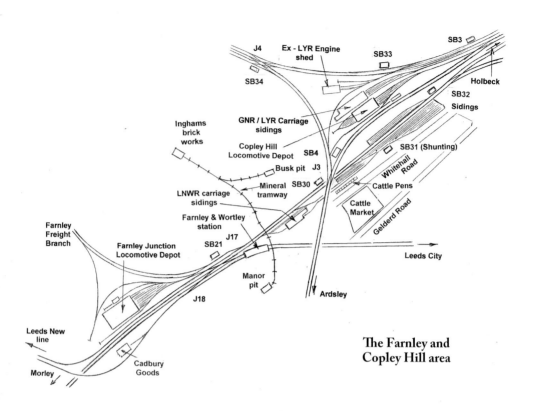

The Farnley and
Copley Hill area

Freight in Leeds, 2009

Very little freight now operates in the Leeds area. Hunslet East handles aggregates from Rystone to Tunstead, with eight trains per week (one direction); Leeds Balm Road also handles aggregates to Tunstead, with six trains per week; and Stourton handles containers for Felixstowe, Southampton and Tilbury, with 36 trains per week. The main freight movements are coal from Scotland to the Aire Valley power stations and containers from Stourton, together with some stone traffic.

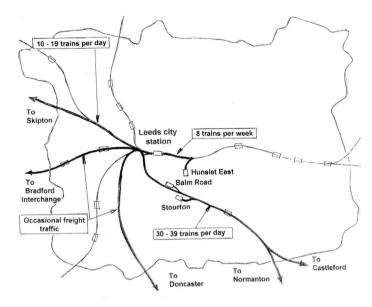

Below: **Leeds Freightliner depot at Stourton opened in 1967 as the only positive outcome of the Beeching Plan. It was built on the site of Stourton motive power depot and today is the only significant rail freight facility within Leeds. The photograph was taken in 2000.** *Author*

Opposite bottom: **A flyover junction was built at the Farnley end of the Leeds New line and opened in 1900. It can be seen in this picture of a Newcastle to Liverpool express taking the new line in 1962, hauled by a Class 40 2,000hp English Electric locomotive, the first main-line locomotives built under the 1955 Modernisation Plan and introduced in 1958. In the centre background can be seen the Cadbury rail-road distribution depot built in the late 1950s and served by a rail siding from the Leeds New line. The depot closed in the 1970s and the track from it was recovered and used on the Embsay & Bolton Abbey Railway.** *Gavin Morrison*

9
Made in Leeds

Leeds was at the forefront of railway and locomotive development. It started in 1795 when Matthew Murray and his partner David Wood, later joined by James Fenton, founded their engineering firm at The Round Foundry in Water Lane, Holbeck. It was here that early locomotives were built, starting with the one in 1812 for John Blenkinsop for use on the Middleton Railway.

The firm ceased business in 1843, but Fenton then took over the Railway Foundry at Hunslet previously owned by Shepard & Todd. This then led to numerous locomotive and rolling stock manufacturers being established in the city – at one time Leeds had the greatest concentration of locomotive builders in the world. These companies manufactured every kind of railway equipment, including main-line, narrow-gauge and industrial locomotives and rolling stock as well as steam and electric trams and all types of road vehicles. In fact, more than 19,000 locomotives were built in Leeds, of which a third were by the Hunslet Engine Company, which was the longest-lived of the Leeds locomotive manufacturers.

The Hunslet Engine Company became Hunslet TPL and in 1990 was awarded a contract by British Rail to build 43 Class 323 electrical multiple units for commuter services in the West Midlands. WYPTE entered lengthy negotiations for a subsequent order to lease 13 Hunslet-built Class 323 trains for the Airedale and Wharfedale electrification, but these foundered. As a result of rail privatisation no further orders were secured and by 1996 the Hunslet works had closed.

Manufacturer	Location of works	Products	Dates
Joseph Booth & Bros	Rodley	Electric, battery and mine locomotives; later concentrated on the manufacture of cranes	1847-1970
John Fowler	Hunslet	Steam trams, steam and diesel locomotives, traction engines	1864-1974
Thomas Green & Son	North Street, Leeds	Locomotives and steam trams; later concentrated on road rollers	1848-1975
Greenwood & Batley	Armley Road	Electric trams, electric trucks and motor cars, mine locomotives	1856-1988
Robert Hudson Ltd	Gildersome	Mainly narrow-gauge railway equipment	1865-1984
Hudswell Clarke & Co	Hunslet	Steam and diesel locomotives	1860-1972
Hunslet Engine Co	Hunslet	Steam, diesel and electric locomotives	1864-1995
Kitson & Co	Hunslet	Steam locomotives	1813-1938
Leeds City Tramways	Kirkstall Road	New building and repair of Leeds tramcars	1897-1957
Leeds Forge	Armley Road	Main-line rolling stock	1873-1930
J. & H. McLaren	Hunslet	Early locomotives, later concentrating on gas and oil engines	1876-1965
Manning Wardle & Co	Hunslet	Steam locomotives	1858-1926
Mann's	Hunslet	Steam carts and wagons	1894-1932
Chas Roe	Cross Gates	Buses and trolley buses	1913-1984
Yorkshire Patent Steam Wagon Co	Hunslet	Steam wagons, steam units for railcars	1901-1937

The main companies and products are summarised below. It is difficult to be precise about dates as there is often confusion about the actual end of manufacture, winding-up, mergers or last deliveries, but the dates given represent the general period of company operation in Leeds.

Joseph Booth & Bros

Located at Rodley, Booth's originally built battery locomotives and railway steam cranes before later concentrating on industrial cranes. A standard-gauge battery locomotive is shown here.

John Fowler

Based at the Steam Plough Works in Hunslet, Fowler built steam and diesel locomotives as well as road traction engines. Here is an early narrow-gauge locomotive.

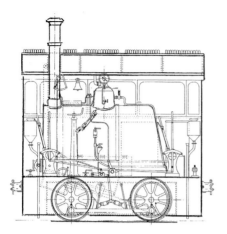
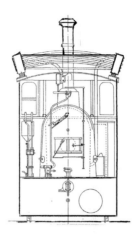

Thomas Green & Son

Formed in 1848 at Smithfield Ironworks in North Street, Leeds, the company built more than 200 steam trams and 36 narrow-gauge steam locomotives before concentrating on the construction of road rollers. This is a Thomas Green steam tram locomotive of about 1890.

What has made Greenbat first choice all over the world? Three factors: **ruggedness, reliability & safety.** Every Greenbat battery locomotive is built to give a lifetime of first class performance under the most arduous conditions. Take the motors, for instance; totally enclosed; weatherproof; windings vacuum impregnated and finished with moisture-resistant varnish; shafts of heat treated alloy steel carried in large diameter bearings; capable of 200% overloads for short periods. The Greenbat range includes 3, 4, 5, 14, and 20 ton models. For full details write to **Greenwood and Batley,** Albion Works, Leeds 12—or 'phone Leeds 20011.

Greenwood & Batley

At its Armley works Greenwood & Batley built electric trams, electric trucks and motor cars before specialising in battery underground and mine locomotives.

Robert Hudson Ltd

Below: **From Gildersome Foundry, Hudson's supplied railway equipment for the complete railway. The company's speciality was tipping wagons, as seen here, mainly narrow gauge but a few for standard gauge.**

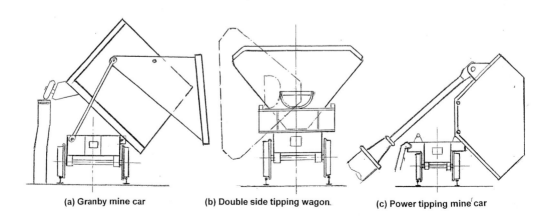

(a) Granby mine car   (b) Double side tipping wagon.   (c) Power tipping mine car

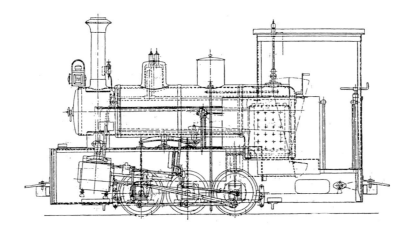

Hudswell Clarke & Co

Top: Based at the Railway Foundry in Hunslet, the company produced steam and diesel locomotives. A narrow-gauge 0-6-0 tank engine is shown here; numerous examples of this type were built for the War Department through Robert Hudson for use in the First World War.

Hunslet Engine Co

Above: Located at Jack Lane, Hunslet was a world-famous builder of steam and diesel locomotives. A Hunslet 0-6-0 saddle tank is shunting Hudson 300cu ft capacity tipping wagons at Peckfield Colliery. These locomotives were Hunslet's most famous product and were adopted as the standard Austerity shunting engine, built in large numbers for use in the Second World war. The train is typical and could be seen at every local colliery carrying spoil from the pit head to the slag heaps. *D. Monkton*

Right: An artist's impression of the Class 323 electric multiple units built by Hunslet in the 1990s for West Midland commuter services.

LOCOMOTIVES CONSTRUCTED BY KITSON & CO. LIMITED.

GREAT NORTHERN RAILWAY.

THE LEEDS FORGE CO., Ltd., LEEDS

MAKERS OF EVERY DESCRIPTION OF

PATENT PRESSED STEEL ROLLING STOCK

(Suitable for any Gauge.)

30-ton All-Steel Bogie Coal Wagon.
(As supplied to Caledonian Ry.)

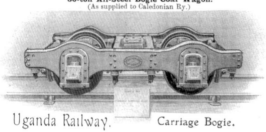

Uganda Railway.   Carriage Bogie.

Kitson & Co

Above: This world-famous builder of steam locomotives operated at the Airedale Foundry until its closure in 1938. A GNR 2-6-0 locomotive is shown.

Leeds Forge

Left: This major rolling stock manufacturer at Armley employed at one time 2,000 people. The company paid its last dividend in 1921 and was bought out by Cammell Laird in 1923, but closed in 1930. Shown here is an example of a typical freight wagon and a pressed steel bogie, which Leeds Forge pioneered.

J. & H. McLaren

Another Hunslet manufacturer, McLaren was located at the Midland Engine Works until moving to the Airedale Works in 1946. The company built two early locomotives but concentrated on the manufacture of gas and oil engines.

Manning Wardle & Co

Left: A major Leeds locomotive builder based at the Boyne Engine Works in Hunslet, it was the first to close in 1926. A narrow-gauge 0-4-0 tank locomotive is shown here.

Mann's

Left: **Mann's built steam cars and wagons at its Hunslet Pepper Road Works.**

Chas Roe

Left: **Famous for building buses at its Cross Gates factory, it also built post-war trams Nos 601 and 602 for Leeds City Tramways.**

Below: **This 0-6-0 diesel-mechanical shunting engine in Holbeck shed in 1935 was supplied to the LMS by the Hunslet Engine Company in 1934, one of three Leeds companies developing diesel shunters at this time, the others being John Fowler and Hudswell Clarke. This type of locomotive was the first to replace steam, as no shunters were included in the BR Standard range of locomotives – diesel shunting engines were built instead.** *Lens of Sutton Association*

10
Leeds city centre railway stations

The railways were one of the largest employers of staff in the city. Of the central Leeds stations, both Wellington and New each had more than 200 staff, with a further 130 at Leeds Central and 60 more at Holbeck. Even suburban stations would have a dozen or so employees to handle passenger and freight traffic. In addition, all the signal boxes had to be manned, some 24 hours a day. Then there were staff at freight depots, train crews and maintenance staff, giving the railways a huge payroll. Similarly, Leeds Tramways had a staff of 3,500 at its peak, of which 2,000 were in the traffic department and more than 300 on permanent way.

As technology on the railways developed the amount of labour was reduced, and as power signalling was extended the number of signal boxes declined. Manpower at local station was also gradually reduced until 1986, when the last local stations were de-manned completely, with fares paid on the train. Today only five local stations have ticket staff: Cross Gates, Garforth, Guiseley, Horsforth and New Pudsey.

Leeds city centre railway stations		
Year	Station	
1834	Marsh Lane	Leeds & Selby Railway terminus
1840	Hunslet Lane	North Midland Railway (NMR) terminus
1846	Leeds Wellington	Leeds & Bradford Railway (via Shipley) terminus, including connection from NMR enabling Hunslet Lane terminus to be closed and converted to goods depot
1848	Leeds Central	Leeds, Dewsbury & Manchester Railway terminus; services later transferred to Wellington/New with GNR and LYR using Central
1855	Holbeck	GNR high-level and NER low-level stations (MR low-level platforms opened 1862)
1869	Leeds New	NER constructed new cross-city line to link up with LNWR with Leeds New station. Original Marsh Lane terminus converted to goods depot with new Marsh Lane station provided on through line
1882		Viaduct line opened, Canal Junction-Farnley North Junction
1938	Leeds City	Wellington and New stations combined to form new City station
1967	Leeds City	Reconstructed to enable Central station to be closed and all passenger rail services concentrated at City
1975		Leeds City renamed Leeds
1987		Viaduct line closed
1998	Leeds	Additional platform W opened to make 13 platforms in total
1999	Leeds Whitehall	Temporary station to facilitate Leeds station reconstruction
2002	Leeds	Further reconstruction by Railtrack to cater for growing traffic; western approach increased from four to six tracks and four extra platforms provided

Marsh Lane

The first station to serve Leeds was on the fringes of the city centre at Marsh Lane. It was used until the North Eastern Railway constructed a new route in 1869, which included a new station on the through line. The old terminal station was then converted into a freight depot.

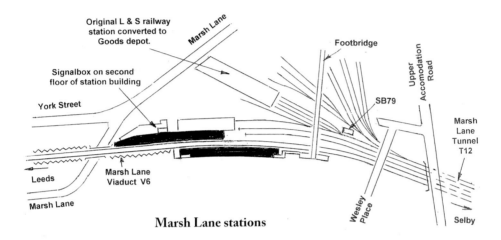

Marsh Lane stations

An old photograph of Marsh Lane station in about 1900, showing a local train bound for Leeds at the staggered platform with the unique but very simple NER-type waiting shelter. Also of interest is the station second-floor signal box; there were two similar ones in Leeds at Stanningley and Tingley. The station was useful for passengers making for the east side of Leeds city centre but was closed in 1958. Just before closure, with a very poor peak-only service, 190 passengers per day still used the station. Today it would be of great value to people had it been retained. *Author's collection*

Hunslet Lane

This was the next station to serve Leeds, but only survived for a few years before its usefulness was reduced by the opening of the new Wellington station. This also later became a freight depot, and a new Hunslet passenger station was provided a few hundred yards south on the through line. For more details of its location see page 116.

Leeds Wellington

In 1846 the Leeds & Bradford Railway opened a new station at Wellington adjacent to City Square; this was the first true Leeds city centre station. Also at this time the North Midland Railway extended its line from Hunslet to the station, which later became the Leeds terminus for the Midland Railway.

Leeds New

In 1869 the NER constructed a new line from Marsh Lane to join up with the LNWR at Leeds Junction. This construction involved the massive clearance of homes, as in those days the population was densely packed around the city centre. The route also ran through a graveyard, resulting in gravestones being relocated on the railway embankment near Leeds Parish Church.

This scheme included a new city centre station called Leeds New, which was jointly built by the two companies. Initially the station only consisted of one through platform with a bay at each end. The station was enlarged again in 1874 and was a considerable engineering feat, being built on arches above the River Aire. The LNWR further improved through services in 1882 with the opening of the Viaduct line, which gave the company a more direct route into Leeds by avoiding running via Holbeck.

The station, which was next door to Wellington station, had ten platforms of which three were through roads to enable cross-city running. Access to and from the through platforms was by a pedestrian subway, later replaced by a footbridge. After this time some alterations were made to the layout of the concourse and a new platform for milk and horse box traffic was added next to Platform 10. On some early maps of the station this is marked as Platform 11 although it is not known if the platform officially carried this number.

A 1932 view of the ex-Midland Railway Leeds Wellington station in LMS days. *Stations UK*

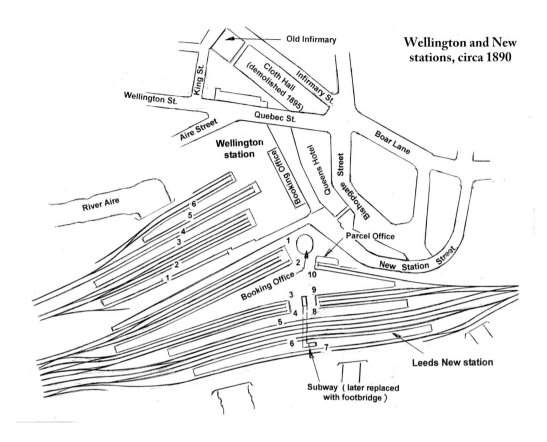

The concourse of Leeds New station in Edwardian times. *Lens of Sutton Association*

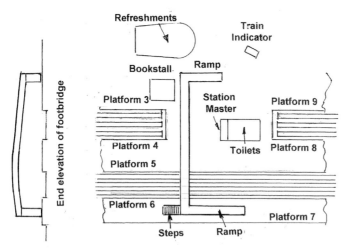

Above: Ex-LYR Aspinall 2-4-2T No 10871 stands at the head of a train of vans at Leeds New station in 1932. These locomotives were used on many LMS local trains at this time. The ugly extension to the train shed can be seen. *Stations UK*

Left: In about 1890 until closure in 1967 a footbridge replaced the original subway at Leeds New station

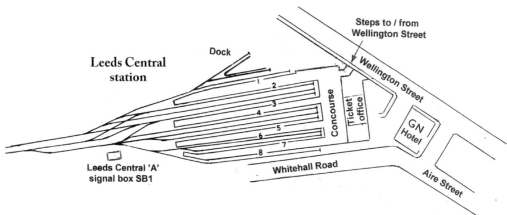

Leeds Central

The Central station at Leeds was first opened as a temporary station in 1848 by the Leeds, Dewsbury & Manchester Railway, followed a year later by the Leeds & Thirsk Railway in an adjoining station. By 1854 Leeds Central had been developed into a main city centre terminal, and was extended in 1904, when it had eight platforms. It was jointly owned by the GNR, LYR, LNWR and NER, but used almost exclusively by GNR, with a few LYR and GCR trains.

Above: Leeds Central survived long enough to see most services diesel-operated. Here Bush Type 4, later Class 47, No D1110 leaves Central with an express train just before closure. *G. W. Sharpe*

Below: The very last passenger train to leave Leeds Central station, the 18.10 to Harrogate, explodes detonators as it departs on 29 April 1967. It is formed by a Metropolitan-Cammell DMU complete with commemorative headboard. The official closure date of the station was 1 May, after which trains were diverted into the enlarged and rebuilt Leeds City station. *John Holroyd*

Holbeck

The station at Holbeck is included as a city centre station as it was close to the city centre and closely connected with the central stations as it was widely used as an interchange station to save passengers the walk between the central Leeds stations. This was a quite unique station, originally called Holbeck Junction in pre-Grouping days. In fact, it was two interconnected stations. It was also important as a parcel exchange point between trains, and by the 1950s this role was considered more important than as a passenger station. The High Level station was used mainly by the GNR, but also by some LYR and GCR trains. Most trains stopped here and it had a staff of 45. The Low Level station was more spartan, with some 120 MR and NER trains per day stopping.

Holbeck was also a thriving community in its own right, with dense housing and excellent transport links. Tramways ran at both sides of the station to the Cattle Market, on the south side until 1922 and on the north side until 1956. Despite the demolition of most of the housing around the station, it survived until closure in 1955.

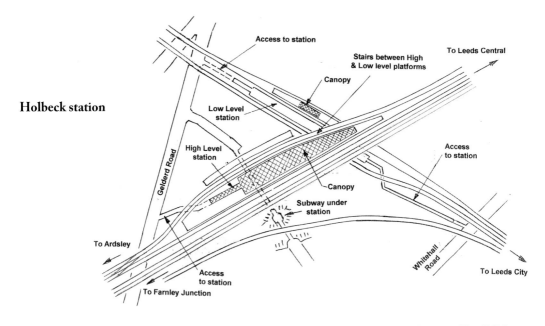

Holbeck station

Looking towards Leeds at Holbeck High Level station in 1932, a local train is headed by LNER 0-6-0 Class 'J3' No 4133. Note the long platforms, as almost all trains stopped at this station, including those to and from London. *Stations UK*

A table showing the morning and evening peak arrivals and departures at Holbeck's High Level (HL) and Low Level (LL) stations in 1910, showing the connection times between trains.

Arrival from		Time		Depart to	Arrival from		Time		Depart to
Bradford via Stanningley	HL	08.34			Bradford MR via Shipley	LL	16.52		
Bradford MR via Shipley	LL	08.37			Harrogate NE	LL	16.56		
Bradford GN via Tingley	HL	08.40					17.03	HL	Liverpool LY Express
Harrogate NE	LL	08.44			Bradford GN via Pudsey	HL	17.04		
Castleford GN	HL	08.45					17.05	LL	Ilkley NE via Arthington
		08.45	HL	Cleethorpes GC			17.08	HL	Wakefield GN
		08.46	LL	Bradford MR via Shipley	London KX GN	HL	17.09		
		08.48	HL	Batley GN via Tingley			17.12	HL	Pudsey GN
Bradford GN express	HL	08.49					17.19	HL	Bradford via Stanningley
Doncaster GN	HL	08.51			Bradford via Stanningley	HL	17.28		
Ilkley NE via Arthington	LL	08.52			Bradford GN via Tingley	HL	17.31		
		08.53	HL	Bradford via Stanningley			17.34	HL	London KX GN
Batley GN via Tingley	HL	08.54					17.34	LL	Ilkley NE via Arthington
Bradford GN via Pudsey	HL	08.57			Pudsey GN	HL	17.38		
		08.58	HL	Barnsley GN via Tingley			17.43	HL	Bradford GN via Tingley
Otley NE via Arthington	LL	09.01			Bradford GN express	HL	17.44		
		09.04	HL	London KX GN	Doncaster GN	HL	17.46		
Harrogate NE	LL	09.11					17.47	LL	Harrogate NE
		09.12	HL	Batley GN via Tingley	Liverpool LY express	HL	17.49		
Doncaster GN	HL	09.18					17.49	HL	Bradford via Pudsey
Shipley MR	LL	09.23					17.53	HL	Batley via Lofthouse
Batley GN via Tingley	HL	09.23					17.55	LL	Ilkley MR
		09.24	LL	Ilkley NE via Arthington	Harrogate NE	LL	17.56		
		09.25	HL	Bradford GN via Pudsey	Bradford MR	LL	17.58		
		09.29	HL	Bradford GN via Tingley			17.58	HL	Doncaster GN

Below: Holbeck Low Level station, seen here looking towards Leeds, was jointly owned by the NER and MR. The station was very cramped and, although an interchange station, not all trains stopped here. It was also used for ticket-collecting purposes and the exchange of parcels. *Transport Treasury*

Inset: Holbeck station was connected by numerous dimly lit passages and alleys, giving it a typical Victorian atmosphere. Here is one of the grim entrances to the station from street level. Many still exist, but are now blocked off; however, a footpath under the station site is still in use today. *Author's collection*

Leeds City, 1938

In 1938 the adjacent but separate Wellington and New stations were combined to become known as Leeds City, and at the same time the north concourse was opened and the present Queens Hotel built. Platforms were renumbered 1 to 16 starting from the Wellington end with No 6 added to the old New station platform numbers. The station trackwork and approaches were resignalled with modern colour lights to replace the semaphore signals.

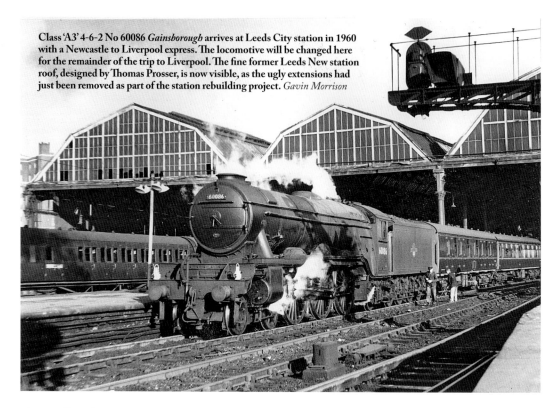

Class 'A3' 4-6-2 No 60086 *Gainsborough* arrives at Leeds City station in 1960 with a Newcastle to Liverpool express. The locomotive will be changed here for the remainder of the trip to Liverpool. The fine former Leeds New station roof, designed by Thomas Prosser, is now visible, as the ugly extensions had just been removed as part of the station rebuilding project. *Gavin Morrison*

Leeds City, 1967

In 1959 British Railways announced a major scheme for Leeds City station that would enable Leeds Central to be closed, with all services concentrated on an enlarged City. Details of the scheme went on public display, and it was to include more through platforms and escalators, as shown in the accompanying track layout. This involved increasing the number of tracks from the west from four to six with a flyover to take London and Bradford route trains over the Holbeck to Aire Valley spur used by freight trains. Work on the scheme started at the end of 1959.

However, in July 1961 the scheme was halted for reassessment. When the project was restarted in 1963 it was in a very much slimmed down form: the basic four-track approach was retained and no flyover was included. The scheme was finally completed in 1967. The north concourse became disused and, although a right of way was maintained through it, this soon fell into disrepair and at one time was used for car parking. The old Wellington part of the station became a parcels depot and was used by parcel and mail trains with an overhead barrow-way connection to the other platforms.

The number of platforms was reduced to 12, but this included two extra through platforms. The old subway was reopened and extended to replace the ramped footbridge and a new stepped overbridge was provided at the east end of the station. A new south concourse was opened as the main access to the platforms, with a small eastern side access directly into New Station Street, although this fell into disuse after a while.

The new scheme rerouted trains from Huddersfield and Wakefield Westgate into Leeds and a new power signal box was opened at Leeds station, resulting in the closure of numerous outlying signal boxes. In 1975 the station became officially known as simply Leeds on nameboards and timetables, although most people continued to call it Leeds City. An economy measure in 1987 resulted in the Viaduct line from Gelderd Junction to Leeds station being closed, forcing trains from and to the Doncaster line to travel again via Holbeck Junction, thus adding to capacity problems. The station track area was electrified in 1990.

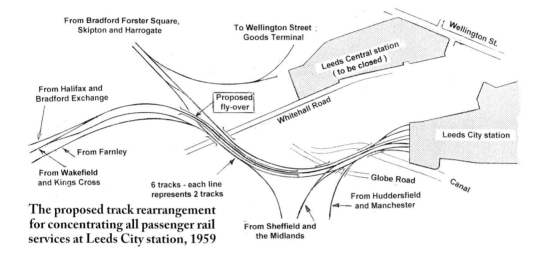

The proposed track rearrangement for concentrating all passenger rail services at Leeds City station, 1959

The 1967 Leeds City station had an unimaginative train shed, and the skyline from the west was dominated by the overhead barrow-ways. A Class 101 DMU forms a train for Blackpool in 1986. *Author*

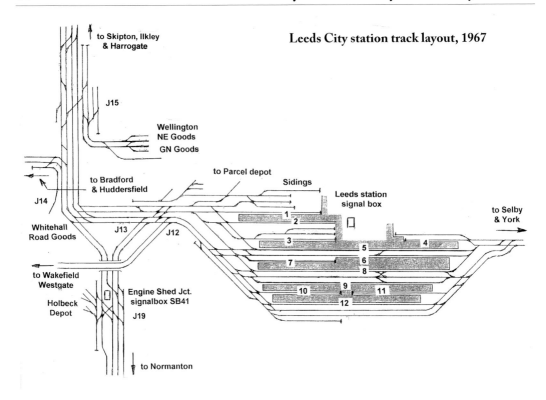

to Skipton, Ilkley & Harrogate

Leeds City station track layout, 1967

J15

Wellington
NE Goods

GN Goods

to Parcel depot

to Bradford & Huddersfield

Sidings

Leeds station signal box

J14

to Selby & York

Whitehall Road Goods

J13   J12

to Wakefield Westgate

Holbeck Depot

Engine Shed Jct. signalbox SB41

J19

to Normanton

Class 45 No 45111 *Grenadier Guardsman* waits to leave Leeds with a departure for Nottingham in 1977. The train is a through service from Glasgow, a remnant of the original Glasgow to St Pancras expresses. This service was itself discontinued in the 1980s. Note the uninspiring but functional 1967 train shed. *Michael Mensing*

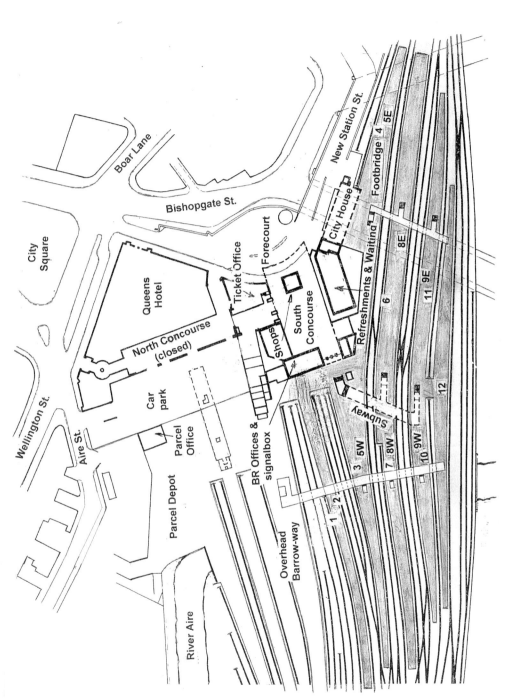

Leeds City station facilities, 1967

Leeds, 1998

By 1990, with large increases in traffic, the station had become very outdated and congested and in 1994 it was taken over by Railtrack, which began to draw up plans to rebuild it. As a prelude to this a new extra platform was built on the site of the old parcels depot; it was very long, could accommodate a London train, and opened in 1998 as Platform W. It later became Platform 1 in the final rebuilding scheme.

Above: **A Class 156 unit forms a train for Carlisle at the new Platform W in 1998. This later became Platform 1 in the final scheme. Between 1998 and 2002 two additional platforms were built between the existing station platforms and the new Platform W.** *Author*

Right: **A Class 142 in Northern Spirit livery stands at Platform W in 1998. These units were a wider and longer version of the Class 141 but with an unimaginative box shape unlike the Class 144 trains. A Class 153 single unit is on the right in the siding on the site of the original Wellington station. When these were used as single-unit trains into Leeds they suffered from severe overcrowding, but were later used to strengthen other units to form longer trains.** *Author*

Leeds Whitehall

The rebuilding of Leeds station was expected to be a major task that would result in widespread disruption. To minimise this a new station was built on the avoiding line at Leeds Whitehall. This enabled night-time Manchester Airport to York trains to serve Leeds without using the main station. Also some suburban trains were terminated here with passengers bussed into the centre of Leeds. The station had full passenger facilities, but was quickly demolished once it was no longer needed.

Above: **A temporary station was erected on the Whitehall curve to facilitate the rebuilding of Leeds station. The first view shows a train for Sheffield in 2001 and the second is the station exterior, showing the extensive station facilities provided. Passengers were bussed between this station and the forecourt of Leeds station.** *Both author*

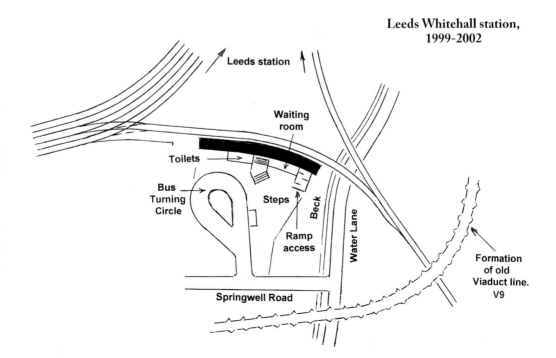

Leeds Whitehall station, 1999-2002

Leeds, 2002

The track layout for the new station was very similar to the one proposed in 1959, with six approach tracks, but this time had 17 platforms, four more than the original plan. Modern escalators and lifts were provided to all platforms Under this scheme the north concourse was returned to its former glory.

A flyover was not included in the western approach tracks but it is believed that the design allowed for this to be added later if required. With completion of this project in 2002 Leeds finally achieved a station worthy of the city.

In 2008 proposals were unveiled for a new south-side entrance. Consideration was also being given to the creation of two additional bay platforms at the west end.

To give an idea of the growth of passenger traffic through the central Leeds stations, in 1903 Wellington saw 236 trains daily, New 299 and Central 237, making a total of 772. (In the same year 300 trains per day called at Holbeck.) In 1969 Leeds City station saw 425 trains daily, and in 2008 Leeds dealt with 1,276. (These are arrivals and departures – through trains are counted as separate trains.)

The rebuilt 2002 Leeds station has more platforms and a modern train shed. A Metro Class 158 unit stands at Platform 15 (previously 12). The 158s were the last class of DMU built by British Railways. On the right a Class 155 is at the new Platform 17; Platforms 16 and 17 were built on the old goods avoiding lines and siding. *Author*

Leeds station and approaches, 2002

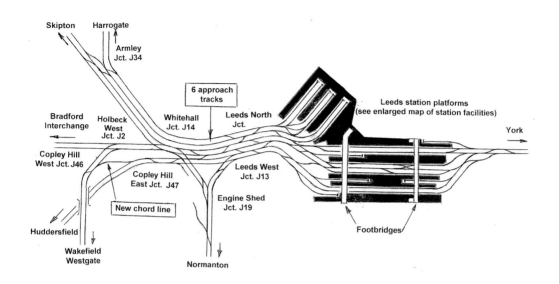

Leeds station train shed profiles, 1848-2002

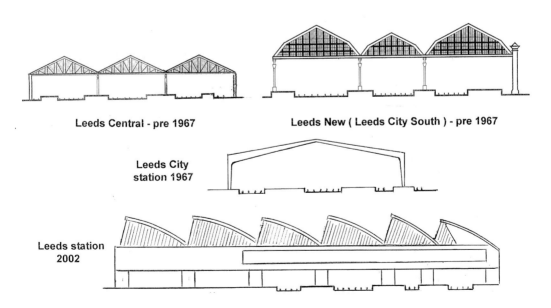

Leeds Central - pre 1967

Leeds New (Leeds City South) - pre 1967

Leeds City station 1967

Leeds station 2002

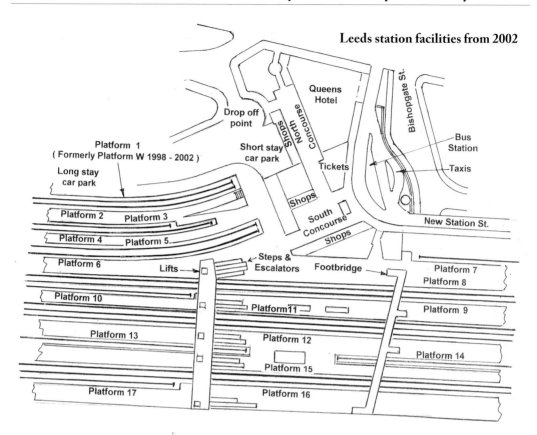

Leeds station facilities from 2002

Automatic ticket barriers

The traditional practice was for tickets to be purchased at station ticket offices and checked manually as passengers passed through ticket barriers at the main stations. In the 1970s British Rail, to reduce costs, started changing to an open station policy with ticket inspection on the train, which had become possible with the phasing out of non-corridor carriages. Tickets continued to be sold at the main stations but most local stations became unmanned and ticket barriers were abolished at most main-line stations. Leeds was one of the few major stations to retain manned ticket barriers but in 2008 these were replaced by automatic ticket gates.

11
Leeds railway infrastructure

Bridges and flyover junctions

Most of the numerous bridges crossing both over and under roads, rivers and canals were quite modest, but there were a number involving extensive engineering works, including the flyover junctions constructed at Beeston Junction by the GNR, Farnley Junction by the LNWR and Kirkstall by the MR. The GNR routes had the most extensive structures, with a large girder bridge at Holbeck station and a massive bridge on the Hunslet branch, which crossed both the River Aire and canal at Thwate Gate.

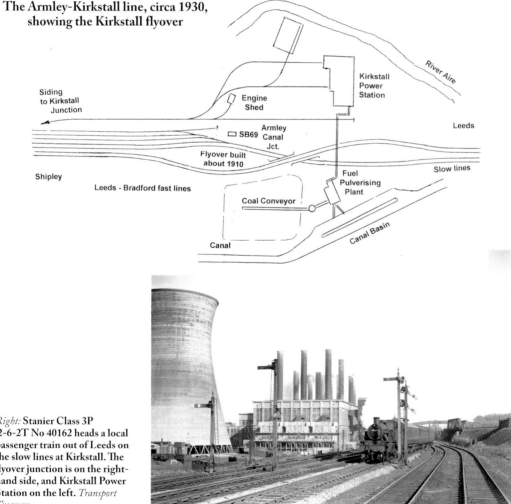

The Armley-Kirkstall line, circa 1930, showing the Kirkstall flyover

River Aire

Kirkstall Power Station

Engine Shed

Siding to Kirkstall Junction

Leeds

SB69 Armley Canal Jct.

Flyover built about 1910

Shipley

Leeds - Bradford fast lines

Coal Conveyor

Fuel Pulverising Plant

Slow lines

Canal Basin

Canal

Right: **Stanier Class 3P 2-6-2T No 40162 heads a local passenger train out of Leeds on the slow lines at Kirkstall. The flyover junction is on the right-hand side, and Kirkstall Power Station on the left.** *Transport Treasury*

**A sketch of the GNR girder bridge over the River Aire
and canal erected in 1899 as part of the Hunslet branch**

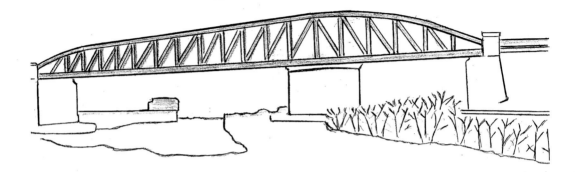

Gradients

Because of the hilly terrain of Leeds most routes are heavily graded. Leeds is in a valley and the Midland routes to both the north and south are relatively flat as they follow the course of the River Aire. The others, apart from the York and Selby routes, involved powerful climbs out of Leeds, particularly with steam power. The steepest gradients were on the closed lines to Tingley and the Leeds New line. Even on routes still open today there are steep climbs out of Leeds to Ardsley, Morley, Bradford and Horsforth, although modern diesel and electric traction makes light of the work

Leeds main-line gradient profiles

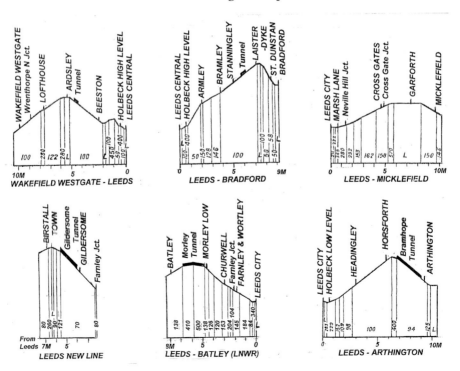

Junctions

On the various maps in this book the junctions are coded with 'J' numbers. The full list is given in the accompanying table.

	Leeds main-line junctions. The 'J' numbers refer to the maps.				
J1	Three Signal Bridge	J17	Farnley North	J33	Micklefield
J2	Holbeck	J18	Farnley	J34	Armley
J3	Wortley South	J19	Engine Shed	J35	Apperley Bridge
J4	Wortley West	J20	Hunslet	J36	Esholt
J5	Beeston	J21	Stourton	J37	Rawdon
J6	Parkside	J22	Methley LY & Mid	J38	Arthington South
J7	Ardsley	J23	Methley	J39	Arthington North
J8	Colliery	J24	Methley South	J40	Arthington West
J9	Tingley East	J25	Bramley West	J41	Wetherby West
J10	Tingley West	J26	Stanningley	J42	Wetherby North
J11	Adwalton	J27	Pudsey	J43	Wetherby East
J12	Canal	J28	Neville Hill	J44	Gelderd Road (created 1967)
J13	Leeds	J29	Waterloo	J45	Farnley Branch (created 1967)
J14	Whitehall	J30	Cross Gates	J46	Copley Hill West (created 2002)
J15	Gelderd	J31	Garforth	J47	Copley Hill East (created 2002)
J16	Copley Hill	J32	Garforth East		

Level crossings

As a result of the terrain and high standard of railway construction very few level crossings existed. The main ones are listed below; there were a few other minor ones, but they were mainly foot crossings. The 'LC' number refer to maps.

LC1 Adwalton Junction
LC2 Methley North
LC3 Thorpe Arch
LC4 Walton Gates

Signals and signal boxes

Following numerous accidents in the early days of railways all the companies developed signalling for the safe running of trains, and as traffic developed more signal boxes were added so that by the end of the 19th century signal boxes were provided at approximately

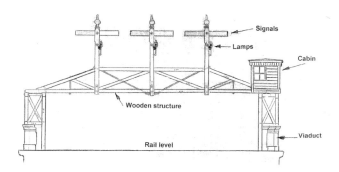

A sketch of an early signal gantry erected by the GNR at the entrance to Leeds Central station in 1855. It was constructed from wood and called the 'Three Signal Bridge'. It was used until 1872 but the name lived on with the signal gantry giving its name to the nearby junction. When Leeds Central station was closed in 1967 the withdrawal notice referred to 'Three Signal Bridge Junction'.

2-3-mile intervals, usually at stations, tunnels or junctions. The signalling operated on the 'block' principle, whereby only one train was allowed in the section between signal boxes. Taken from old maps, the accompanying table shows the main-line signal boxes in use in Leeds in about 1900 (there were some other small colliery branch boxes not listed). Generally most signal boxes survived until the 1950s.

\multicolumn{8}{c}{**Leeds signal boxes. The 'SB' numbers refer to the maps.**}							
SB1	Leeds Central 'A'	SB21	Worley & Farnley	SB41	Engine Shed Junction	SB61	Horsforth	SB81	Waterloo Junction
SB2	Leeds Central 'B'	SB22	Gildersome LNWR	SB42	Hunslet Junction	SB62	Bramhope Tunnel	SB82	Killingbeck
SB3	Holbeck	SB23	Wards Sidings	SB43	Hunslet South	SB63	Arthington South	SB83	Cross Gates
SB4	Wortley South	SB24	Morley Low	SB44	Pepper Road	SB64	Arthington North	SB84	Manston
SB5	Beeston Station	SB25	Leeds Wellington	SB45	Wakefield Road	SB65	Pool in Wharfedale	SB85	Garforth Junction
SB6	Beeston Junction	SB26	Leeds New	SB46	Stourton Junction	SB66	Otley	SB86	Garforth East Junction
SB7	Parkside Junction	SB27	Leeds Canal Junction	SB47	Rothwell	SB67	Wortley Junction	SB87	Peckfield Colliery
SB8	Hunslet GNR yard	SB28	Leeds Junction	SB48	Robin Hood	SB68	Armley Station Junction	SB88	Micklefield
SB9	Ardsley North	SB29	Whitehall Junction	SB49	Rothwell Haigh	SB69	Armley Canal Junction	SB89	Kippax
SB10	Ardsley West	SB30	Copley Hill No 1	SB50	Waterloo C Sidings	SB70	Kirkstall Junction	SB90	Allerton Main
SB11	Ardsley Station	SB31	Copley Hill No 2	SB51	Woodlesford	SB71	Kirkstall Forge	SB91	Ledston
SB12	Ardsley South	SB32	Copley Hill No 3	SB52	Methley	SB72	Newlay & Horsforth	SB92	Scholes
SB13	Spring Lane	SB33	Wortley East	SB53	Methley Junction	SB73	Calverley & Rodley	SB93	Thorner
SB14	Lofthouse Sidings	SB34	Wortley West	SB54	Methley LY	SB74	Apperley Bridge Junction	SB94	Bardsey
SB15	Tingley	SB35	Armley Station	SB55	Gelderd Junction	SB75	Esholt Junction	SB95	Collingham Bridge
SB16	Woodkirk	SB36	Bramley Station	SB56	Wortley NE	SB76	Rawdon Junction	SB96	Wetherby West
SB17	Morley Top	SB37	Bramley West Junction	SB57	Armley NE Junction	SB77	Guiseley	SB97	Wetherby North
SB18	Gildersome GNR	SB38	Stanningley	SB58	Cardigan Road	SB78	Leeds City East	SB98	Wetherby East
SB19	Adwalton Junction	SB39	Pudsey Lowtown	SB59	Headingley	SB79	Marsh Lane	SB99	Thorpe Arch
SB20	Drighlington Station	SB40	Pudsey Greenside	SB60	Horsforth Woodside	SB80	Neville Hill Junction		

In 1937 the LNER introduced modern colour light signalling at Leeds New station. Three old mechanical signal boxes, Leeds New, West and Canal Junction, were replaced by a new Leeds City Station West signal box.

With the closure of Leeds Central in 1967 and reduced traffic levels, the trackwork in the whole Leeds area was rationalised and resignalled to concentrate all services at the rebuilt Leeds City. Numerous signal boxes were closed and colour light signals extended over a wider area, controlled from a new signal centre on the fifth floor of the Leeds station building.

Subsequently modern signalling was gradually extended further afield, but in 1999 expanding rail traffic made it necessary for Leeds station to be rebuilt. In 2002 Railtrack commissioned the new Leeds station signalling with the entire area now controlled from York; the only Leeds signal box to remain is that at Horsforth.

Opposite above: **A Leeds to Sheffield local train formed by a Class 101 DMU in white and blue refurbished livery passes under a signal gantry at Pepper Road, Hunslet, in 1978.** *Author*

Above: **A Class 185 Trans-Pennine unit forms a Leeds to Manchester express as it passes a colour light signal near White Rose on a snowy day in 2009.** *Author*

Right: **Type 2 diesel locomotive (later Class 25) No D5177 passes Methley South signal box as it comes off the Methley Joint line with a coal train from Newmarket Colliery in 1970. The line was jointly owned by the GNR, LYR and NER and, although closed to passenger traffic in 1960, part of the route was retained for coal traffic.** *M. Mitchell*

The track layout of the railways of Leeds remained practically unchanged for 50 years until the major changes of the 1960s. The scheme to close Leeds Central station involved major alterations to rail routes into Leeds from 1967. The 'fringe' boxes to the new Leeds power signal box are shown.

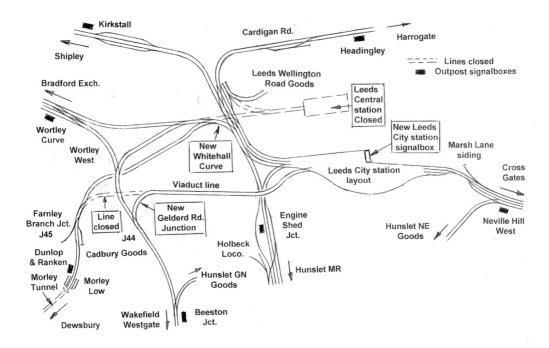

Below: A new Gelderd spur and junction was provided to give an alternative route for trains from London, which was used for 20 years until closure in 1987. A Leeds to London train joins the original line at Gelderd Road Junction just before closure of the Viaduct line. *Author*

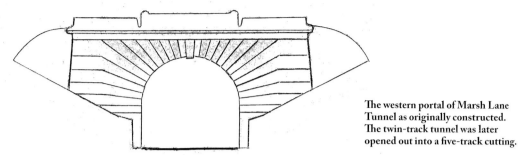

The western portal of Marsh Lane Tunnel as originally constructed. The twin-track tunnel was later opened out into a five-track cutting.

Tunnels and viaducts

Tunnels and viaducts in Leeds are listed in the accompanying tables, together with the tunnel lengths in kilometres.

Leeds tunnels and their lengths (km). The 'T' numbers refer to the maps.	
T1	Apperley Lane (0.068)
T2	Ardsley (0.270)
T3	Armley (0.082)
T4	Bramhope (3.438)
T5	Gildersome Street (0.140)
T6	Gildersome (2.130)
T7	Green Bottom (Guiseley) (0.123)
T8	Greenside (Pudsey) (0.563)
T9	Headingley (0.056)
T10	Hill Foot (0.414)
T11	Hindles (0.029)
T12	Marsh Lane* (0.640)
T13	Morley (3.070)
T14	Spring (0.070)
T15	Woodkirk (Soothill) (0.602)
* Tunnel later widened and opened out as a cutting	

Leeds viaducts. The 'V' numbers refer to the maps.	
V1	Arthington
V2	Churwell
V3	Kirkstall
V4	Leeds Central
V5	Leeds New station
V6	Marsh Lane
V7	Stanningley
V8	Tingley
V9	Viaduct Line

A Manchester-bound DMU emerges from the western portal of Gildersome Tunnel in 1964. When I lived at Gildersome this is the spot where, after a walk over the fields, we could watch the trains on the Leeds New line. I also travelled on this line a number of times from Manchester, and it was easily the quickest route between Huddersfield and Leeds. Today this line would be of great benefit in providing much-needed extra capacity and quicker journey times as the Class 185 units would have made easy work of it. Gildersome Tunnel remains unused, and a possible potential asset to be used again? The Government is now looking at High Speed Line 2, which would link all the urban areas of Britain from London to Birmingham and Manchester, then Leeds to Newcastle and Scotland. The tunnel could possibly form an entry to Leeds through the watershed. *M. Mitchell*

Left: A Leeds-bound express crosses Churwell Viaduct in early BR days hauled by an ex-LMS 'Jubilee' locomotive. Note the rural setting before the area became built up. Churwell station was immediately to the right of the six-arch viaduct. Most Leeds viaducts have survived either by still being in use or preserved as a reminder of our industrial heritage. *Morley History Society*

Left: Demolishing Leeds railway infrastructure: in the decade from 1959 billions of pounds worth (at present-day values) of rail infrastructure was destroyed in the name of progress. Goods and passenger stations were demolished with even the platforms removed, four tracks were reduced to two, junctions were eliminated and the large Leeds tramway system was abandoned. Here we see demolition taking place at Kirkstall station just after closure. *Transport Treasury*

Below: All this was done with great haste and with no regard for possible future use. Opposition and alternative views were brushed aside as the 'powers that be' had no foresight other than catering for the motor car. This is Farnley Junction shed in February 1967 following closure the previous year. The track has been removed and the shed, water tower and coal plant await demolition. *D. K. Jones*

12
A-Z of Leeds suburban railway stations

I have many memories of Leeds suburban railway stations. About 1950 the picture was one of well-kept stations, quite infrequent services, high fares and, as a result, quite modestly used services. We lived directly behind Gildersome station and I was thus able to witness first-hand the running of the station. The service offered was very restricted, consisting of an obscure Lofthouse to Drighlington peak-hour shuttle service mainly tailored to the miners who worked at the Lofthouse and East Ardsley collieries. You always knew of the arrival of the colliery train as the loud noise of the miners' clogs could be heard. It was push-pull-operated and worked by an Ivatt Class 'C12' tank locomotive. However, as a service this was

Railway staff gather at Gildersome station in May 1962 to mark the retirement of Mr Leonard Wood after 51 years of service. Mr Wood was Station Master for many years and a personal friend of my father, who was dispatch foreman at Robert Hudson Ltd, the local firm that was the main customer at Gildersome station. Incidentally, my father had a permit from British Railways to walk along the railway to his employment. Note that even seven years after closure the station is still intact, although a little overgrown. *Stephen White/Leslie Overend*

not much help to other passengers, although in theory changes could be made at Ardsley for Leeds and Wakefield. My father did occasionally take me on the local service to Leeds, changing at Ardsley; it was reasonably quick but the high fares deterred use.

In 1952 we moved to Morley and I frequently used the Low station and occasionally Morley Top. I remember on one occasion using the London train at Top station for a trip to Doncaster. Again the fares were very high, but the service was much better with quick journeys from the Low station to Leeds and Huddersfield. The station was well kept and,

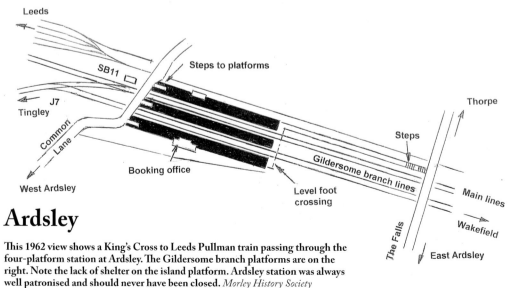

Ardsley

This 1962 view shows a King's Cross to Leeds Pullman train passing through the four-platform station at Ardsley. The Gildersome branch platforms are on the right. Note the lack of shelter on the island platform. Ardsley station was always well patronised and should never have been closed. *Morley History Society*

being at the mouth of the tunnel, was a very interesting place to visit. Shortly afterwards the station area became very run-down with the demolition of the adjacent hotel and surrounding houses, which isolated and blighted the whole area for years to come. The station retained its gas lighting until the end of the 1960s, making alighting from the steam-hauled 11.08pm Leeds to Huddersfield train very atmospheric.

A favourite trip was to catch the bus to Ardsley, walk down Common Lane, then take the train to Castleford. The station at Ardsley was a hive of activity, being on the main line and surrounded by marshalling yards and the locomotive depot.

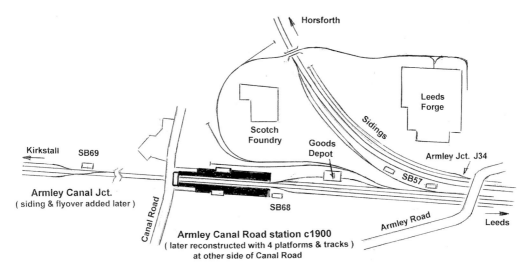

Armley Canal Road

The former MR station, seen here looking towards Shipley in 1963, previously had two platforms on the opposite side of Canal Road, as shown in the map of about 1900. In the 1900s the whole Midland route was converted to four tracks, with all stations provided with four platforms, except Kirkstall Forge, which was closed. *Stations UK*

My grandparents lived at Osmondthorpe overlooking the station, but despite trying I was never able to use the station due to a very restricted peak-only service. We did, however, use the excellent station at Cross Gates for trips to Scarborough by catching the tram as a feeder.

Another station I used was Bramley, where my wife came from. It was very similar to Morley with a proud old station being gradually run down, then closed.

Generally speaking I used most of the local train services from Leeds, in particular to Ilkley, York and Normanton. I have happy memories of these, but it is sad how such fine suburban stations could be run down and closed when they had such great potential to be developed. In the following pages we will look at all the suburban stations of Leeds and remember the fine railway infrastructure that we once had.

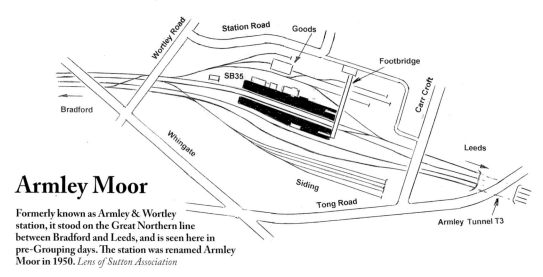

Armley Moor

Formerly known as Armley & Wortley station, it stood on the Great Northern line between Bradford and Leeds, and is seen here in pre-Grouping days. The station was renamed Armley Moor in 1950. *Lens of Sutton Association*

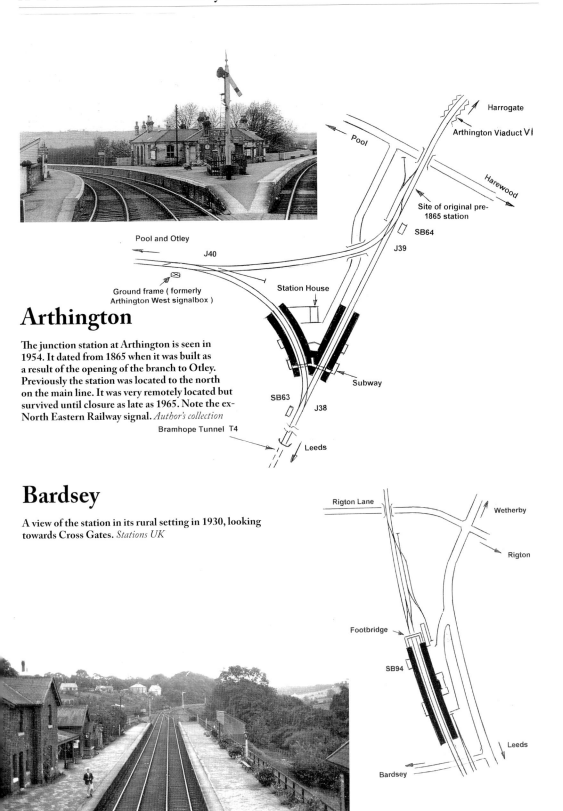

Arthington

The junction station at Arthington is seen in 1954. It dated from 1865 when it was built as a result of the opening of the branch to Otley. Previously the station was located to the north on the main line. It was very remotely located but survived until closure as late as 1965. Note the ex-North Eastern Railway signal. *Author's collection*

Bardsey

A view of the station in its rural setting in 1930, looking towards Cross Gates. *Stations UK*

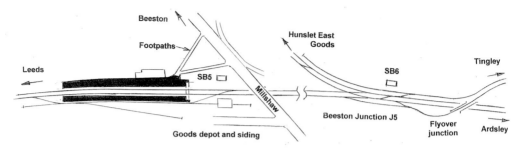

Beeston

A local train of corridor coaches hauled by Class 'N1' 0-6-2T No 69447 approaches Beeston station from Leeds in 1956. The station had closed in 1953 but was retained for use by football supporters travelling to Elland Road, when trains were specially stopped on match days. *Author's collection*

Bower Halt

Bower Halt was erected in 1934.

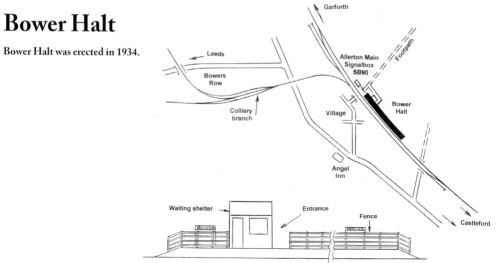

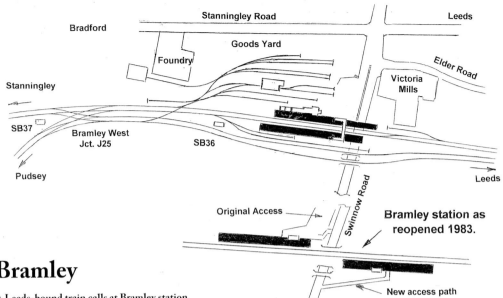

Bramley station as reopened 1983.

Bramley

A Leeds-bound train calls at Bramley station in 1966, just before closure. Four tracks are still in place but it can be seen that rationalisation has taken place, although the water tank required for steam trains still survives. The map shows both the original station circa 1900, and as reopened in 1983
D. K. Jones

Burley Park

A train for Leeds formed by a Class 141 unit arrives at Burley Park station in 1988 shortly after its opening. *Author*

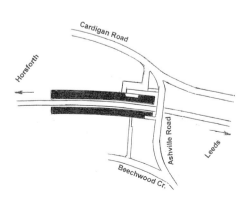

Calverley & Rodley

Note in this early picture looking towards Leeds the extensive station buildings; the stations on this line were built to a lavish scale with four platforms being provided for both the fast and slow lines. *Lens of Sutton Association*

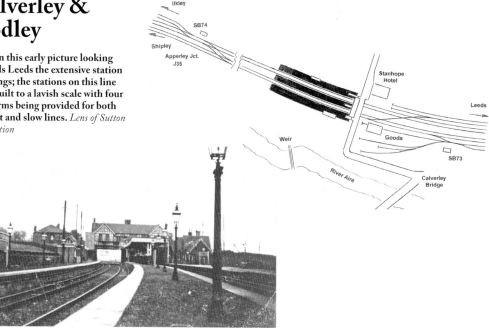

Churwell/Cottingley

Below left: The first picture shows Churwell station looking towards Leeds. It was located on a viaduct and closed as a wartime economy measure, officially in 1940, although local sources indicate that it actually closed a year earlier. WYPTE did look at reopening a new station on the same site, but it was considered that piling of the embankment would be necessary and Cottingley station was opened instead.

Below right: The second photograph shows a single-car Class 153 unit forming a Huddersfield to Leeds service at Cottingley station in 2000. The Class 153 trains were formed by splitting two-car Class 155 units into two separate single cars for lightly used services. However, following the growth in rail patronage these are now frequently recoupled together to become two-coach trains again. *Author's collection/author*

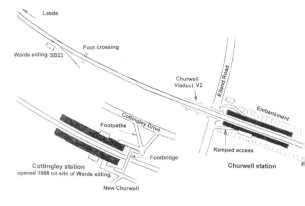

Collingham Bridge

Brand new 'Peak' Class (later Class 46) locomotive No D188 passes Collingham Bridge station in 1962 with a Newcastle to Liverpool express via Wetherby. Note the station goods yard on the right, which was used to stable the empty stock of special trains to Wetherby races. *M. Mitchell*

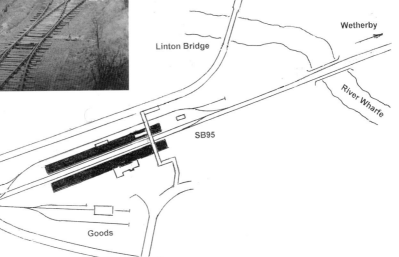

Cross Gates

A Manchester to Scarborough train calls at Cross Gates station in 1987. It can be seen that the previous four tracks and junction have been reduced to two plain tracks. *Author*

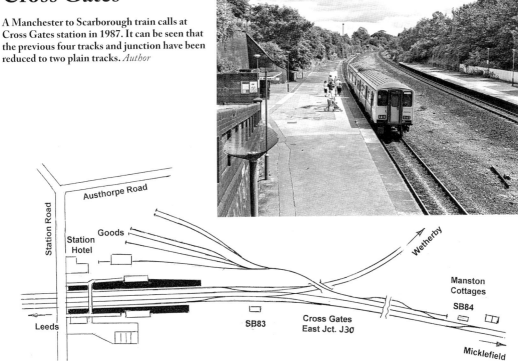

Drighlington & Adwalton

This 1938 view taken from the signal box is looking towards Wakefield. An ex-GNR train is possibly waiting for the signals to clear at Adwalton Junction for Wakefield via Batley. These trains were replaced by a short-lived DMU service before closure in 1962. *Stations UK*

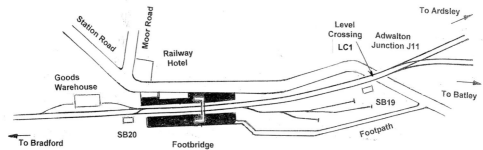

East Garforth

A Class 150 DMU calls at the newly opened East Garforth station in 1987. The unit is new and has not yet received its all-over yellow ends for safety and high visibility. The WYPTE introduced cross-Leeds local trains, and this is a Manchester to Selby service. *Author*

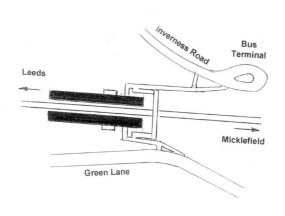

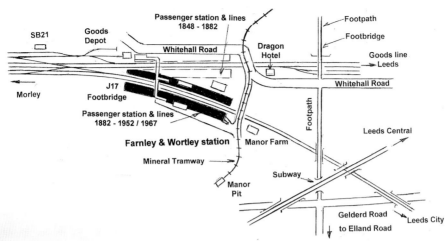

Farnley & Wortley

This is the view from the footbridge in LMS days in 1932. The extensive buildings and canopies of the station can be seen. The bridge in the centre of the picture carried a mineral tramway and path and gave access to the south side of the station. After closure the station was retained for a number of years for football supporters to reach Elland Road football ground, when scheduled trains were stopped specially. *Stations UK*

Garforth

A York to Bradford local train picks up passengers at Garforth station in 1977. Garforth was a former pit village but the station and rail service benefited from major residential development. To cater for this WYPTE introduced cross-Leeds local train services from York and Selby to Bradford and opened a new station nearby at East Garforth. The map is circa 1900. *Author*

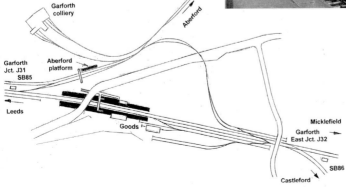

Gildersome (GNR)

This view in GNR days is looking towards Bradford. The large booking office can be seen and to the left is the unusually tall signal that train drivers were able to see before they entered the far end of the 156-yard-long Gildersome Street Tunnel. The tunnel was built by the 'cut and cover' method and ran directly under Gildersome crossroads. I remember in about 1949 workmen changing the GNR signals for the more modern upper-quadrant semaphore type. *Morley History Society*

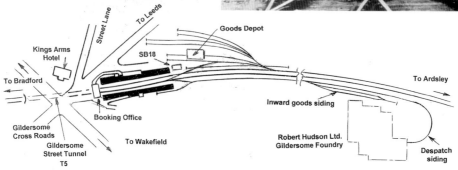

Gildersome (LNWR)

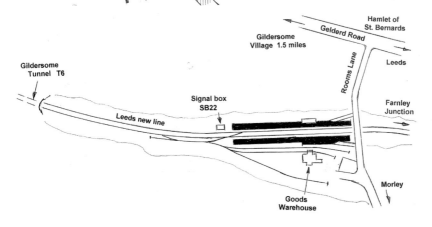

There are no known photographs of this short-lived station, but the ends of the platform can just be seen by the signal box. The sketch shows how the station may have looked. It was very isolated with more than a mile of uphill walk to the village. In fact, it was nearer to parts of Morley via Rooms Lane. The station was lightly used but it can be seen that it was very neat and accessible, and would put many modern stations to shame. *Morley History Society*

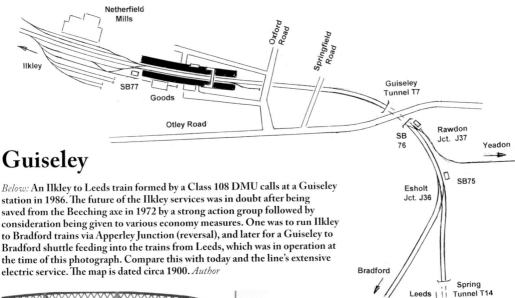

Guiseley

Below: An Ilkley to Leeds train formed by a Class 108 DMU calls at a Guiseley station in 1986. The future of the Ilkley services was in doubt after being saved from the Beeching axe in 1972 by a strong action group followed by consideration being given to various economy measures. One was to run Ilkley to Bradford trains via Apperley Junction (reversal), and later for a Guiseley to Bradford shuttle feeding into the trains from Leeds, which was in operation at the time of this photograph. Compare this with today and the line's extensive electric service. The map is dated circa 1900. *Author*

Headingley

Right: A Leeds to Knaresborough train calls at Headingley station in 2008. The station is well used but suffers from poor facilities. Access to the Leeds platform is by a steep spiral staircase and connecting paths are quite poor and isolated. *Author*

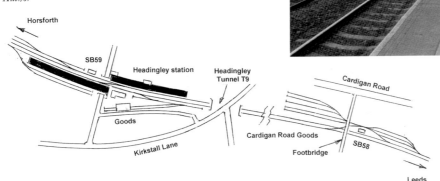

Horsforth

A Horsforth to Leeds train calls at Horsforth in 1978. The train is formed by a Class 101 unit that has been refurbished to extend its life and is in the white and blue livery intended for services in provincial PTE areas. *Author*

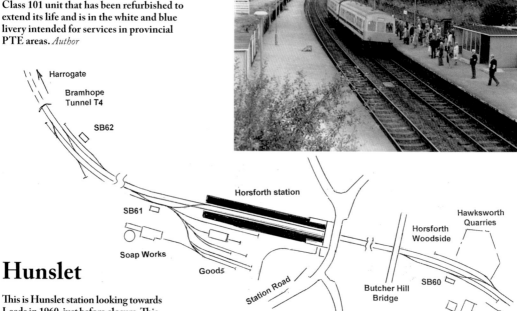

Harrogate

Bramhope
Tunnel T4

SB62

Horsforth station

SB61

Hawksworth
Quarries

Horsforth
Woodside

Soap Works

Goods

Station Road

Butcher Hill
Bridge

SB60

Horsforth
Brick Works

Leeds

Hunslet

This is Hunslet station looking towards Leeds in 1960, just before closure. This station only had two platform faces with goods lines behind. It was opened in 1873, being the third station after the closure of the original Hunslet Lane terminus and a short-lived station on the main line a few hundred yards further south. *Author's collection*

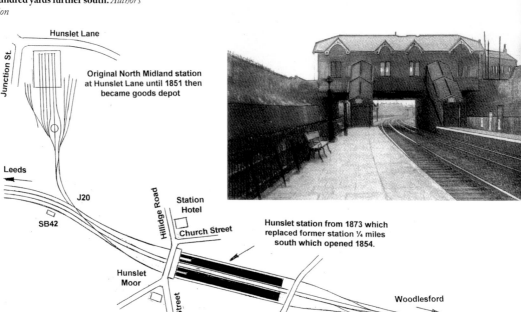

Hunslet Lane

Junction St.

Original North Midland station
at Hunslet Lane until 1851 then
became goods depot

Leeds

J20

SB42

Hillidge Road

Station
Hotel

Church Street

Hunslet station from 1873 which
replaced former station ¼ miles
south which opened 1854.

Hunslet
Moor

Beza Street

Woodlesford

SB43

Middleton Railway

Kippax

This view of the single-platform station is looking towards Castleford in pre-Grouping days. Note the well-laid-out gardens. In fact, the photograph is marked '1st prize', suggesting that it was taken for a best-kept station competition, which were very popular in those days to encourage well-looked-after stations. *Lens of Sutton Association*

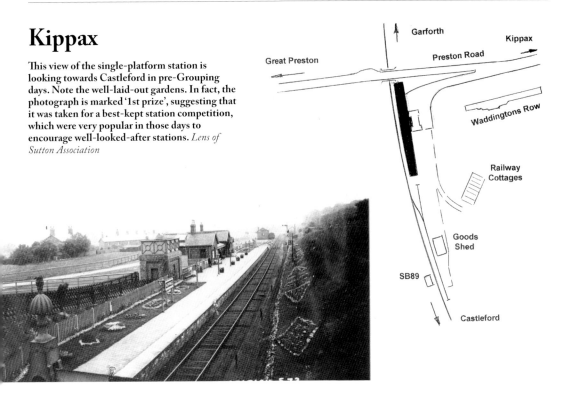

Kirkstall

A local train for Leeds calls at Kirkstall station in pre-Grouping days. Both the train and station buildings have Midland Railway brandings and the noticeboard carries adverts for trips to an Agricultural Show in Hull and to Birmingham and Gloucester. *Lens of Sutton Association*

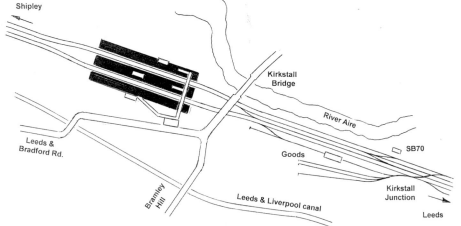

Kirkstall Forge

This station was built to serve the famous engineering works of the same name, but was an early casualty and closed in 1905, about the time the line was being widened from two to four tracks, after which it continued to be used as a goods depot. The are no known photographs of the station, but the station building survived for many years and is shown here. Ironically the works have now closed and the site has been cleared to be redeveloped for housing, including a new railway station. The map is dated circa 1900. *Author's collection*

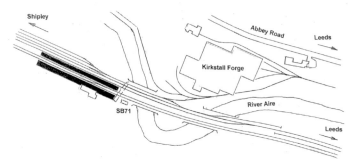

Ledston

Diesel locomotive (later Class 37) No D6916 passes through Ledston station in 1971 with a coal train. The station is still intact despite being closed for many years. Allerton Bywater Colliery is on the left, with a branch stub being retained from Castleford to cater for coal traffic from this and Primrose Hill Colliery. *M. Mitchell*

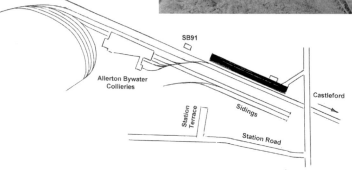

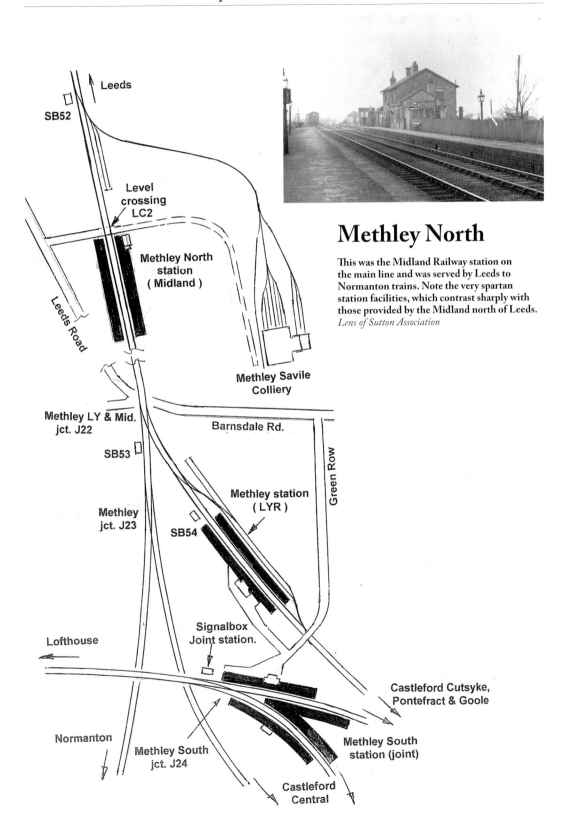

Methley North

This was the Midland Railway station on the main line and was served by Leeds to Normanton trains. Note the very spartan station facilities, which contrast sharply with those provided by the Midland north of Leeds.
Lens of Sutton Association

Leeds

SB52

Level crossing LC2

Methley North station (Midland)

Leeds Road

Methley Savile Colliery

Methley LY & Mid. jct. J22

SB53

Barnsdale Rd.

Green Row

Methley jct. J23

SB54

Methley station (LYR)

Methley South jct. J24

Lofthouse

Normanton

Signalbox Joint station.

Castleford Cutsyke, Pontefract & Goole

Methley South station (joint)

Castleford Central

Methley (LYR)

A view of the remains of the dilapidated station in 1956, 13 years after closure. *Stations UK*

Methley South

This is the joint GNR/LYR/NER railway station at Methley Junction. It was used mainly by the ex-GNR Leeds Central to Castleford Central service using the platforms on the right. Here we see one of the many freights that used these lines. *Stations UK*

Micklefield

Below: **A Liverpool to Hull Trans-Pennine express train passes Micklefield station in 1979; it is formed by a Class 124 Intercity DMU specially built for this service and introduced in 1961. The station buildings have since been demolished to reduce the station to an unmanned halt. The map shows the station in about 1900.** *Author*

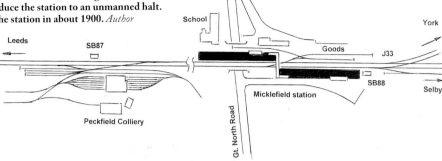

Morley Low

Above: **The ex-LNWR station at Morley, situated at the mouth of Morley Tunnel, was renamed Morley Low by BR in 1952 to distinguish it from the ex-GNR station, which became Morley Top. Here a Class 101 DMU forms a train for Leeds on a Bank Holiday Monday in 1979. The station was de-manned in 1986 and the signal box closed when control of the tunnel was transferred to Batley signal box. The hillside to the left of the station was the site of Morley Main Colliery, which was open from 1854 to 1909 and is seen in the circa 1900 map. At its peak in 1883 it employed more than 1,000 men and boys. A disaster at the pit in 1872 killed 34 miners.** *Author*

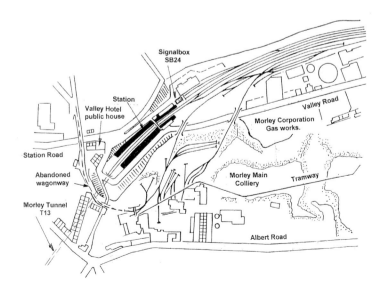

Morley Top

Below left: This is the station in Great Northern days, viewed from the Wakefield direction. The signal box in the background was later replaced by a brick structure. The station was close to the town centre via Great Northern Street. Through trains to and from London King's Cross stopped here as three- or four-coach Bradford portions were attached/detached from the main Leeds trains at Wakefield Westgate. *Morley Historical Society*

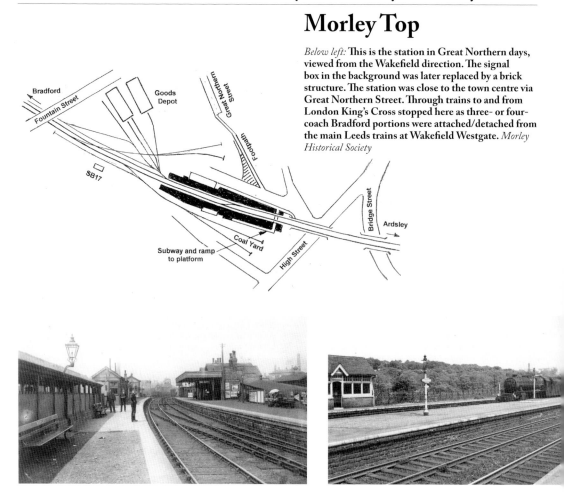

Newlay & Horsforth

Above right: The station had extensive facilities provided by the Midland Railway and was typical of others on the line, with four platforms. Looking east in 1963, a Class 5 locomotive calls with a train from Leeds. *Stations UK*

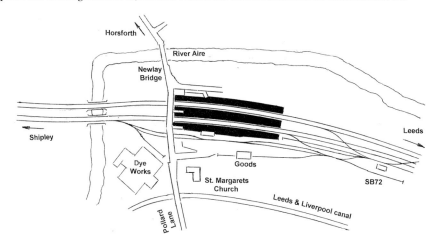

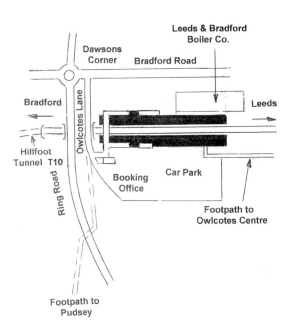

New Pudsey

A two-car Class 110 DMU calls at New Pudsey station in 1986 with a Manchester Victoria to Leeds service. These trains were originally built as three-car units for the Calder Valley Trans-Pennine service, but with a decline in patronage in the 1970s the middle car was removed as an economy measure. *Author*

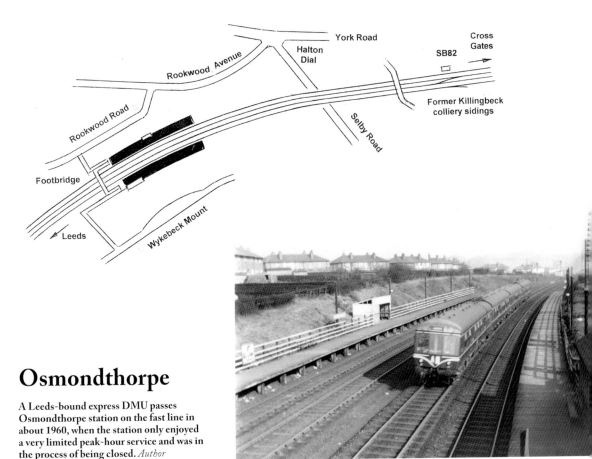

Osmondthorpe

A Leeds-bound express DMU passes Osmondthorpe station on the fast line in about 1960, when the station only enjoyed a very limited peak-hour service and was in the process of being closed. *Author*

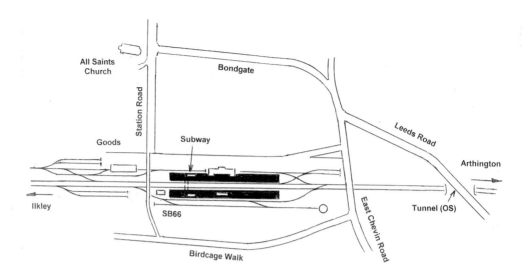

Otley

A local train headed by an ex-LMS Class 3P 2-6-2 tank locomotive enters Otley station in 1959. The station was closed in 1965 as a result of the Beeching 'axe'. Note the large area of railway land; soon after closure most of this was taken for construction of the Otley bypass road. *G. W. Sharpe*

Penda's Way

This view of the halt is looking towards Wetherby in 1961. The station was opened in 1939 to serve large-scale housing development in east Leeds; it was reported that it was built by the LNER in a day, although the foundations had been prepared previously. *Stations UK*

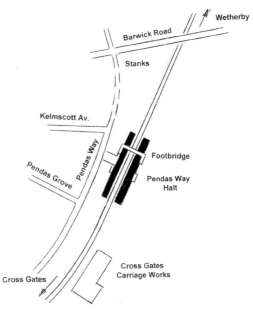

Pool in Wharfedale

A local train from Arthington pulls into Pool in Wharfedale station in 1960. The station closed as a result of the mass shutdown of services in 1965 due to the implementation of the 1963 Beeching proposals. *Author's collection*

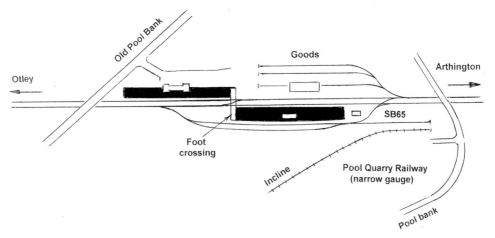

Pudsey Greenside and Lowtown

Right: Pudsey had two stations on the Pudsey loop line opened by the GNR in 1878. The first photograph shows Pudsey Greenside station in 1963 looking towards Leeds. This station had both freight and passenger facilities.

Below: The other station at Lowtown only catered for passengers. This view shows the station looking towards Leeds in 1964, the year that both Pudsey stations were closed. *Both Stations UK*

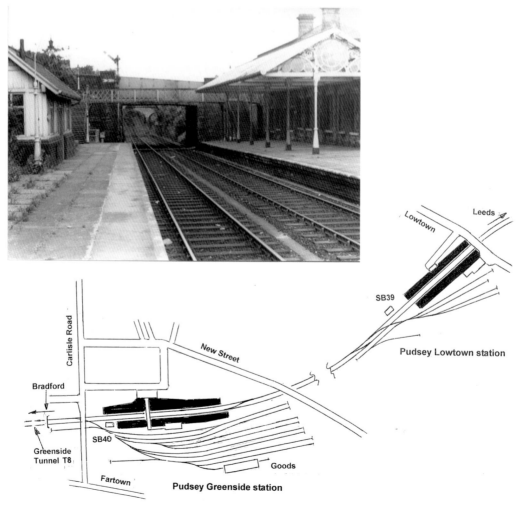

Robin Hood

This view looking towards Leeds shows the single platform of the former EWYUR station at Robin Hood in 1963, almost 50 years after the last regular passenger train ran. The buildings and signal box are still intact and the station continued to be used by excursion trains. *Stations UK*

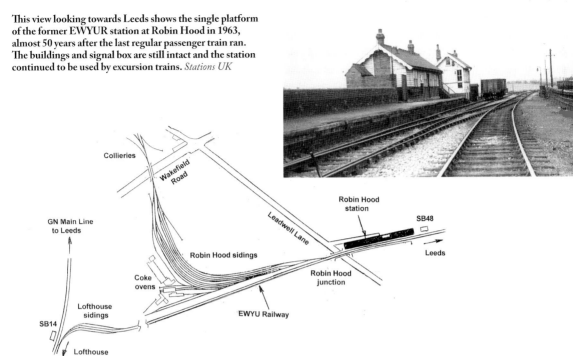

Rothwell

The passenger service only lasted a few months in 1904. This was for two main reasons, first that it had difficulty competing with the electric tramways, and second that the trains terminated at Robin Hood rather than running through to Wakefield. As at Robin Hood, excursion trains used the station for many years. *Author's collection*

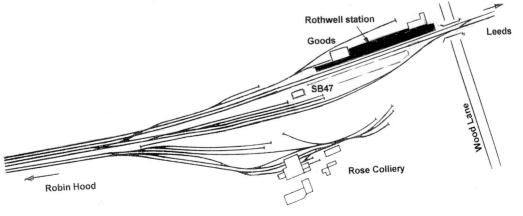

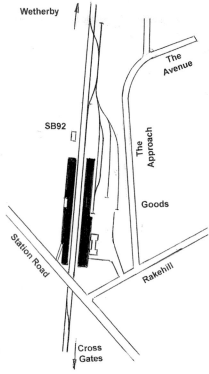

Scholes

This is the view looking towards Cross Gates in pre-Grouping days. It can be seen that there has been a heavy fall of snow and the platforms have been cleared. The main station buildings are on the Leeds-bound platform, with a typical NER waiting shelter on the other. *Lens of Sutton Association*

Stanningley

Until the Pudsey loop was built this was the station for Pudsey, but even after the loop opened the station continued to have a good service with some LYR expresses stopping there. In 1967 the station was replaced by New Pudsey to cater for motorists, but for others the new station was much less accessible from Pudsey than this one. Note the second-floor signal box on the left. *Transport Treasury*

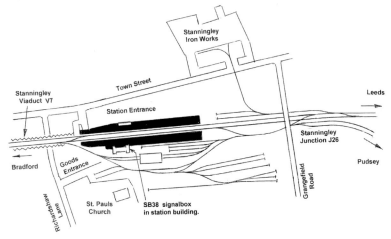

Stourton

There are no known photographs of the EWYUR railway station at Stourton. It consisted of an island platform reached by a subway. The passenger service was very short-lived but, unlike the stations at Rothwell and Robin Hood, it was demolished a few years after withdrawal of the passenger service and replaced with a siding by 1919. The map is dated 1904.

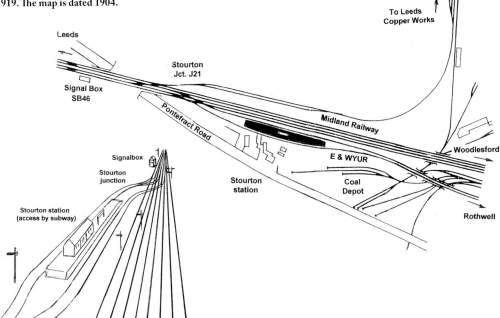

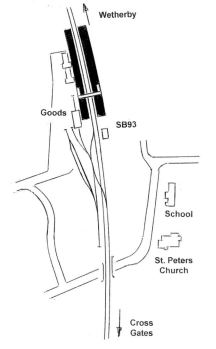

Thorner

This view of is looking towards Wetherby in 1930. The station buildings and waiting shelter are similar to most other stations on the line.
Stations UK

Thorpe Arch

In this 1950s view of the station, level crossing and signal box a Class 'B1' locomotive heads a Church Fenton-bound train. The Ordnance factory was behind the photographer. *Author's collection*

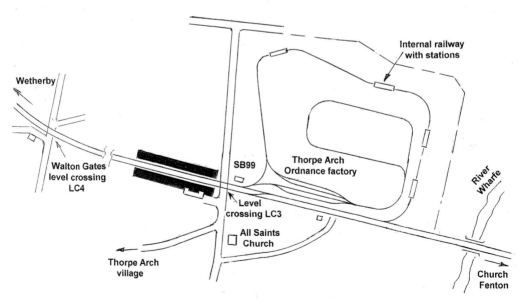

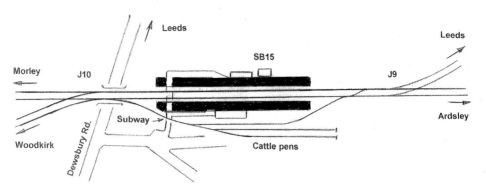

Tingley

Right: We are looking towards Ardsley in GNR days. Note again the second-floor signal box in the station building. *Morley History Society*

Wetherby

Below: The original Wetherby station was on the Church Fenton line, but was converted into a goods depot in 1902 when a new west curve was built and the town's station relocated. Wetherby Racecourse station, seen here in the first photograph, was open from 1924 to 1959 and catered for special trains for the race meetings, which were held about six times each year.

The second photograph is a post-war view of Wetherby station looking from the south. Note the parked cars, from which car enthusiasts should be able to date the picture. Was this one of the first 'park and ride' stations in the Leeds area? This is a service that should never have been withdrawn; had it survived there is little doubt that it would today be very well patronised. *Stations UK/Transport Treasury*

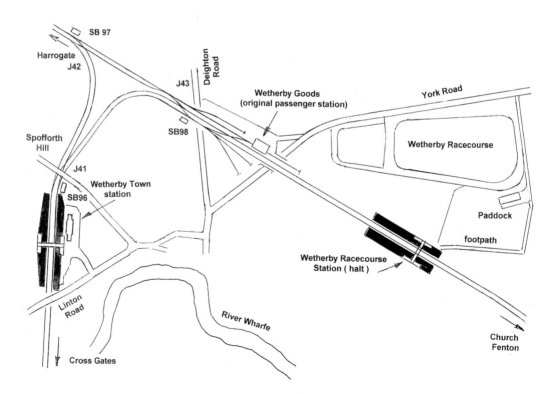

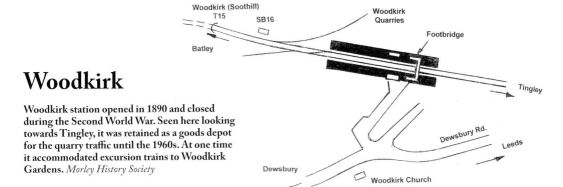

Woodkirk

Woodkirk station opened in 1890 and closed during the Second World War. Seen here looking towards Tingley, it was retained as a goods depot for the quarry traffic until the 1960s. At one time it accommodated excursion trains to Woodkirk Gardens. *Morley History Society*

Woodlesford

A Sheffield to Leeds train calls at Woodlesford in 1987. It can be seen that the original station buildings (see in the circa 1900 map) have been demolished to reduce the station to a basic halt with brick shelters. About this time the station was under threat of closure from an unlikely source, Metro, which proposed diverting the trains from Castleford and Normanton to Leeds via Wakefield Westgate. *Author*

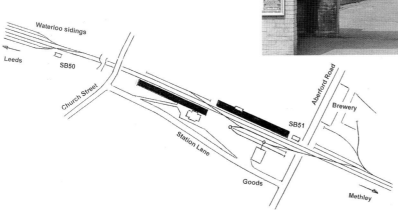

Yeadon

Yeadon station opened in 1894 but never had a regular passenger service. It was planned by a local company that ran into financial difficulties during construction and as result was taken over by the Midland Railway before opening. It was, however, used by excursion trains and prospered as a short freight branch until closure in 1964. *Author's collection*

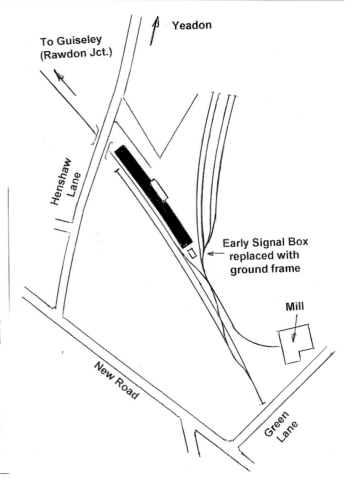

MIDLAND RAILWAY.

OPENING

OF

YEADON BRANCH

The Midland Railway Company hereby give notice that the

NEW LINE TO YEADON

will be opened for

GOODS, COAL, COKE, AND LIME TRAFFIC,

On Monday, Feb. 26, 1894.

Enquiries respecting Rates, &c., may be made of the Station-Master, at Yeadon; Mr. HULL, Guiseley; Mr. JOSEPH SHAW, Mineral Manager, Derby; or of Mr. W. E. ADIE, Goods Manager, Midland Railway, Derby.

GEO. H. TURNER, General Manager.

Derby, February, 1894.

13
Transport policies since 1945

After the Second World War both the city tramways and railways were in a very run-down condition. Although a number of tram routes were planned for abandonment, the future was still seen as being based upon a basic modernised tram network that would use up-to-date single-deck railcars running in city centre subways and on suburban reserved tracks The subway scheme is considered in the next chapter. Despite these plans, the abandoners won the day and the trams finally disappeared from the streets of Leeds in 1959 to be replaced by buses.

On the railways there had been a gradual run-down of the less viable stations and services, but by the end of the 1950s the situation had stabilised and at long last services were being modernised with the introduction of diesel trains to replace steam traction. In addition, in 1959 a major scheme for Leeds City station was announced that would enable Leeds Central to be closed.

However, nationally transport policy was about to change. Conservative Government Transport Minister Ernest Marples, who incidentally had road-building interests, appointed a Dr Beeching as Chairman of British Railways with the brief to conduct a review of the future of the railways in a bid to make them pay. His report was published in 1963 and advocated wholesale closure and abandonment of both freight and passenger traffic. This became Government policy, which now favoured road transport and road-building against a background of railway closures.

What happened to local railways was now dictated by national policy, and the Leeds area suffered savagely from the Beeching cuts, which advocated only six suburban railway stations remaining (see chapter 5). Leeds was now almost totally dependent on cars and buses for its mobility.

In the same year the Government published a report by Professor Buchanan entitled *Traffic in Towns.* In this, Leeds was used as an example of how a town centre could be developed to accommodate the motor car, and the proposals are shown in the accompanying map. This involved the mass demolition of property and the creation of a Motorway Box around the central area. The report was accepted by the Government but criticised locally. Thankfully it was never implemented, but it showed the bias of national policy. One good feature was the creation of pedestrian zones, and shortly afterwards, in 1965, Leeds City Council started the process of converting many city centre streets to give priority for pedestrians.

Two further important reports were published in 1969 that reinforced this road-biased policy. In August came the West Yorkshire Transportation Study, commissioned by West Riding County Council, local councils, the Ministry of Transport, British Railways and the municipal bus companies. It was based upon 1966 travel habits and as a result its findings mirrored the 'Beeching' thinking; its public transport recommendations are shown in the sketch overleaf. These incorporated the core services retained by Beeching, although no funding was available for development, but new services were to be provided by express buses. In October the 'Leeds Approach' was published. This was another joint effort by Leeds City Council and the Ministry of Transport and again the report rejected rail transport in favour of bus rapid transit. The report's forecast of commuting into Leeds by 1981 was bus 70%, car 17.5%, rail 5.2% and other (walking, cycling etc) 7.3%. Unfortunately the bus services failed to attract this level of commuting and the plan was a dismal failure, as shown by the fact that by 1990 70% of commuters were coming into Leeds by car rather than bus.

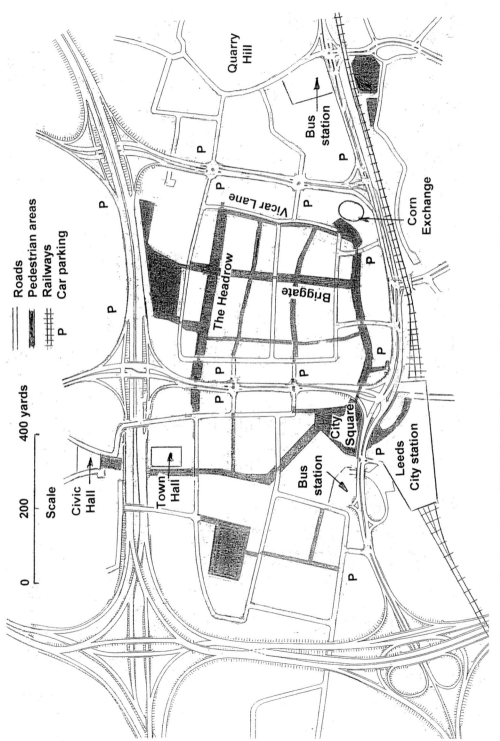

Traffic in Towns (HMSO, 1963): the possible development of Leeds city centre.

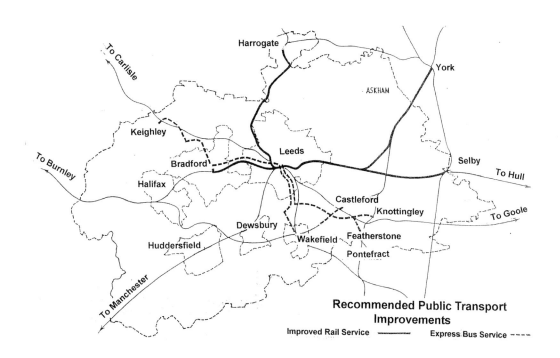

West Yorkshire Transportation Study, 1969: recommended public transport improvements.

These figures confirmed that Leeds was now 'putting all its eggs in one basket' in becoming dependent on road transport alone. All the previous planning of reservations for tramways and railway development was now abandoned in favour of massive road-building.

Local Government was reorganised in 1974, which extended the city boundary of Leeds; more importantly, it created a new Passenger Transport Executive for West Yorkshire, charged with the responsibility of providing and improving public transport in the new county. The new body soon indicated that it saw the potential for improving rail services; it took over financial responsibility for local trains and began a programme of improvements.

By the 1980s it had become perfectly clear that it was a mistake to have abandoned the tram network and a number of attempts have since been tried to reintroduce a modern light rail system to Leeds, as detailed in the next chapter. A decade later patronage on local trains had grown rapidly and railway development was now back on the agenda.

In 2009 a new Transport Act changed the name of the West Yorkshire Passenger Transport Authority (WYPTA) to West Yorkshire Integrated Transport Authority (WYITA). Metro continues as the Executive arm of the new ITA with stronger powers to plan, develop and integrate transport over the Leeds City Regional area. The expectations are that rail will have a central role in developing future transport for the area. Tram-Train is seen as having great potential to radically improve urban transport in the Leeds conurbation.

14
Failed schemes

1945: tramway subways

Subways had been considered before the war, but in 1945 Leeds City Council drew up a detailed scheme to put the city centre tramways underground. The proposal is shown in the accompanying map, and consisted of east-to-west cross-city routes with trams from the south running at a deeper level round an underground loop line under the River Aire.

Originally it was planned to put the subways under city streets using the 'cut and cover' method of construction, but this proved to be impractical and was later changed to bored 'tubes'.

The subways were to be worked by single-deck tramcars with trailers. In 1944 Leeds bought from Sunderland Corporation a single-deck tram for possible future subway use. It was rebuilt to make it suitable for underground operation and numbered 600. Two further cars, Nos 601 and 602, where constructed by Chas Roe and entered service in Coronation year 1953 in a purple and cream livery.

Understandably, with a shortage of money after the war, there was difficulty in implementing the scheme, but the project remained on the books for a number of years. Had the tramway network been retained, a similar arrangement could have been carried out but with trams running on the surface rather than in subways. This would have followed continental practice with motor traffic excluded from much of the city centre, as is the case today. This would have given Leeds a superb modern transit system.

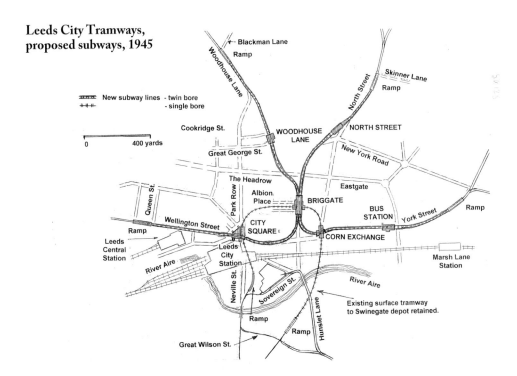

Leeds City Tramways, proposed subways, 1945

1961: Stourton marshalling yard scheme

In 1961 the North Eastern Region of British Railways received approval from the Ministry of Transport to build a new marshalling yard at Stourton. This was planned to handle north-south freight traffic and sort 3,500 to 4,000 wagons per day, replacing 14 smaller yards. Construction work started and a flyover and extensive earthworks were completed before the scheme was abandoned.

1965-1974: bus rapid transit

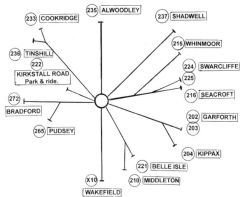

Post-tramway transport planning and the 'Leeds Approach' advocated a bus rapid transit system for Leeds with the normal stage services supplemented by a network of express buses and a 'park and ride' scheme in Kirkstall Road. By

Leeds 'Fastaway' bus rapid transit network, 1965-74

1973 this was in place and the express bus routes are shown in the diagram. The buses used were modern single-deck types and quite a good service was operated, but unfortunately it could not attract motorists from using their cars and the services withered away while the earlier 'park and ride' scheme was very short-lived.

1987: Metro-Line light rail

It was now becoming clear that the abandonment of the trams had been a major mistake and thoughts were turning to reintroducing a light rail scheme. This was considered by a transport study in 1977 when an East Leeds route was considered with a line reserved for a tramway to Seacroft, Cross Gates and Colton, where a major housing development was to take place around the proposed tramway. A joint scheme by the WYPTE and Leeds City Council was announced in 1987.

However, the project provoked strong opposition from people living in the new houses at Colton, who claimed that the tramway came too close to their homes and as a result they would need to be 'underpinned', this despite the route being protected for some time. As a result Leeds City Council axed the scheme during the public consultation period.

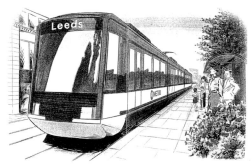

Metro-Line light rail scheme for East Leeds, 1987

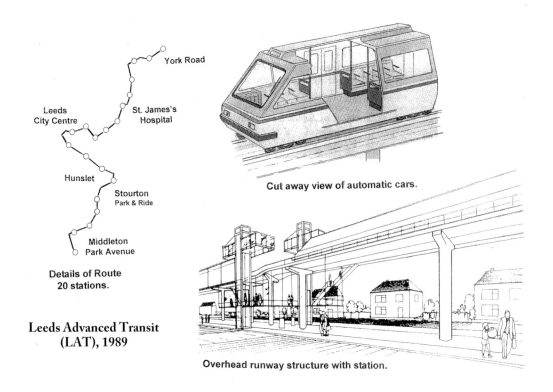

York Road

Leeds
City Centre

St. James's
Hospital

Hunslet

Stourton
Park & Ride

Middleton
Park Avenue

Details of Route
20 stations.

**Leeds Advanced Transit
(LAT), 1989**

Cut away view of automatic cars.

Overhead runway structure with station.

1989: Elevated LAT transit

Two years later Leeds City Council came up with a replacement scheme called Leeds
Automatic Transit. This was certainly far-reaching, but it was as impractical as it was
environmentally unacceptable. The scheme consisted of small automatically controlled
vehicles running on an elevated structure with a route from South Leeds through the
city centre to East Leeds. The route and details of the cars and structure are shown in the
accompanying diagrams. This was never going to happen and was soon abandoned after
wasting two years on the planning process.

1993: Supertram

Following these continuing failures, Leeds City Council next carried out a major transport
study to determine the way forward, and this resulted in the publication of the Leeds Transport
Strategy. One of the main recommendations of this was that a Supertram network should
be built in the city. This resulted in the 1993 Leeds Supertram Act, which authorised the
construction of South Leeds tramway routes from Tingley and Stourton to Leeds city centre.

Metro immediately applied for Government approval, and joined the queue for
funding. By the end of the decade this had still not been received, but as the new century
arrived there was a Labour Government in London that indicated that it wanted to
invest in major light rail schemes, and encouraged Leeds to build a full network instead
of a single route. As a result Leeds now submitted a scheme for a full network to the
Government for approval.

Leeds Supertram, 1993

The Government approved funding for the scheme in 2001 and it was now full steam ahead to build the long-awaited tramway for Leeds. However, this was not to be. In 2004 the Government put the scheme 'on hold' because of concern at rising costs. In a bid to rescue the project the Tingley branch was axed. Despite meeting Government rules and the cost increase being held to 40%, the scheme was finally refused by the Government in 2005, despite four years of planning and millions of pounds spent.

The Government suggested that Leeds should instead invest in buses rather than trams. It was back to square one, and Department for Transport interference in local Leeds transport issues continued.

New and reopened railway stations

In 1986 plans were announced for a new station at Elland Road to cater for football fans. Funding was agreed, but the station never materialised. In the 1990s British Rail wanted to build a station to serve the White Rose Shopping Centre and Office Park, and the developer agreed to fund it. At the same time the WYPTE proposed the reopening of the station at Armley Moor and announced its intention to local residents. Both these schemes floundered because of rail privatisation and escalating costs. In 1999 new stations were back on the agenda, and the WYPTE announced plans to reopen stations at Kirkstall and Horsforth Woodside. After ten years these stations still remain to be opened. Despite the enormous environmental advantages of rail and the fact that the Leeds suburbs are poorly served by rail, it is now 22 years since a new railway station was opened in the city.

15
Tram-Train

Following the collapse of the Supertram project, in 2007 Metro proposed that a Tram-Train scheme could be the way to improve local rail services in Leeds. The idea was that trams would run on suburban railway tracks from outlying areas and, when nearing the centre of Leeds, would veer off and run through the city centre as street tramcars.

The practicality of shared track running has been proved on the Tyne & Wear Metro and in Germany. Lines considered suitable for this type of running are the Harrogate and Castleford lines into Leeds. In the Leeds City Centre action plan there was a proposal for a city centre Tram-Train loop line, as shown in the diagram. A possible branch from Horsforth to Leeds & Bradford International Airport has also been suggested.

The present difficulties with developing the existing railways within Leeds are the general shortage of capacity due to the greater number of regional and long-distance trains and a lack of platform capacity at Leeds station. Tram-Train overcomes these difficulties by using separate street stations for city centre operation. Additionally, more suburban stations can be provided at closer spacing.

Such a system is also very flexible as future extensions can be either railway- or street-based. This brings together both railways and tramways and would be an appropriate way to develop the spare infrastructure that still exists in Leeds.

In 2008 the Government approved a trial of a Tram-Train scheme, which was initially to be on the Sheffield to Huddersfield railway, but in 2009 this was changed, with a trial between Sheffield and Rotherham instead. New vehicles are to be built, with the concept tested for feasibility of operation on conventional railways. It is anticipated that this will prove successful and that a scheme can then be prepared for Leeds.

Tram-Train proposals, 2007 (from the Leeds City Centre action plan by Leeds City Council/WYPTE)

A German Tram-Train